The Boston Globe

MW00738084

# Dining Out

## 52 REVIEWS OF BOSTON'S TOP RESTAURANTS

Published by *The Boston Globe*

# The Boston Globe

**The Boston Globe Store**
PO Box 55819
Boston, MA 02205-5819
Phone: (888) 665-2667
Fax: (617) 929-7636
www.BostonGlobeStore.com

Printed in U.S.A.
ISBN 13: 978-0-9790137-7-5

*The factual information listed in this guidebook was confirmed at press time,
but is subject to change. We therefore recommend that you call ahead or
visit each restaurant online for the most up-to-date prices, menus, and other
information. Reviews reflect the experiences and opinions of the writers, which
may or may not match reader experiences and opinions.*

**EDITOR** Janice Page
**DESIGNER** Rena Anderson Sokolow
**ASSISTANT EDITOR** Devra First
**WRITERS** Alison Arnett, Devra First
**PRODUCTION** Eric Anderson
**ILLUSTRATION** Jerome Layman

**SPECIAL THANKS** The Boston Globe Living/Arts Department;
Nancy Callahan, MacDonald & Evans.

**COVER PHOTO** Jody Adams, chef-owner of Rialto in Cambridge,
displays a tray of freshly shucked oysters. Photo by Yoon S. Byun,
The Boston Globe.

B  O  S  T  O  N     •     C  A  M  B  R  I  D  G  E

**WHAT'S FOR DINNER?** In and around Boston, the answer is "just about anything you want." And that's just what you get in this edition of "Dining Out: 52 Reviews of Boston's Top Restaurants." Of course, 52 is just the tip of the iceberg. In the following pages you'll find reviews of New England and American classics long associated with the area, as well as seasonal bistros, little neighborhood gems with big ideas, and much more. Chowder? It's here, of course. But the true stars of the current restaurant scene speak to the diversity of Greater Boston. ❖ Things are constantly changing on the dining scene, and that's been especially true in recent months. L'Espalier bid adieu to its longtime brownstone location and reopened in modern new digs adjacent to the Mandarin Oriental hotel. Another of the area's best restaurants, Craigie Street Bistrot, is also on the move. (Because of these changes, neither is included in this year's "Dining Out.") Haute Japanese restaurant o ya was named the most intriguing new restaurant outside of New York by the Times. Lumiere's Michael Leviton launched Persephone in the burgeoning Fort Point Channel area. Wellesley favorite Blue Ginger expanded, Locke-Ober's Lydia Shire went Italian with Scampo in the Liberty Hotel, the city was hit by a shabu shabu craze, and football fans got fine dining with the opening of a new Davio's at Patriot Place. ❖ That's a lot to keep tabs on. And that's where this book comes in, offering honest assessments of eateries from the moderately priced to the high-end, including new favorites and classic Boston institutions. Half of the reviews offer my take, and half are penned by longtime Boston Globe restaurant critic Alison Arnett. (I took over the beat in August 2007.) In this guide our reviews combine to tell you what's good — and not-so-good — about a wide variety of local places. ❖ Each review recommends specific dishes (menus are always changing, however), evaluates service, and generally lets you know what you're in for. A star rating is assigned to each restaurant. Four stars is extraordinary, three excellent, two good, 1 fair, and zero poor. For anyone who's ever wondered where to go for that big anniversary celebration, where to take out-of-town visitors or kids, or, perhaps most important, where to dine during a crucial Sox game, we hope "Dining Out" will be an invaluable guide.

DEVRA FIRST, *Restaurant Critic*, THE BOSTON GLOBE

SOMERVILLE • BEYOND

# TEN TABLES

★★★☆

WEEK
**1**

*597 Centre St., Jamaica Plain*
*617-524-8810*
*www.tentables.net*
*MasterCard and Visa accepted.*
*Restaurant wheelchair accessible,*
*restrooms not.*

**PRICES** *Appetizers: $7-$10.*
*Entrees: $18-$25. Dessert: $7.*

**HOURS** *Mon-Thu 5:30-10 p.m.,*
*Fri-Sat 5:30-10:30 p.m., Sun 5-9 p.m.*

**NOISE LEVEL** *The buzz of happy*
*conversation and good music.*

## MAY WE SUGGEST

Charcuterie plat du jour; sea scallops;
duck breast; culotte steak; vegetarian
tasting menu.

TASTING NOTES

_____

_____

_____

_____

_____

**THIS IS A VALENTINE.** Ten Tables, I have a thing for you. Always have, always will. I know I'm not alone in that — you have many suitors, and I have to fight for my fraction of your attention. No, you say, I can't see you this Saturday night. Nope, not next Saturday either. And if five friends and I want to see you together, we'll have to beseech you eons in advance. But maybe you can fit me in at 9:30 p.m., or on a Monday, and I will be glad. After all, you do only have 10 tables. I get that. ❖ It's always worth the wait. You're so cozy, a little box full of good smells. When the lights are down low, jazz is playing softly, the chefs in the open kitchen are laughing, plating, drizzling, and the aroma of creamy celeriac soup or culotte steak is wafting over our heads, it's easy to see looking around the tiny room that you make diners feel good. ❖ It would be hard for them not to, considering what's on the table. Plump, rosy little slices of duck breast edged in spice rub make one see things through rose-colored glasses. Culotte steak is all meat, no fat, striated slivers of beefy bliss. Charcuterie is made in house — wonderful pates and sausages. Seared scallops are everything seared scallops should be — and more, because they're served on nutty, toothsome farro, with tiny red squares of beets scattered throughout like confetti. On top is a Meyer lemon salsa with green olives. ❖ And when meat steps out of the way altogether, I have some of my finest moments with you, Ten Tables. It's hard to think of a better way to spend $28 than on your vegetarian tasting menu. Four courses! For 28 bucks! I'm mentally comparing that to single dishes I've eaten recently that cost more, and I have to laugh. The satisfaction-to-dollar ratio comes out overwhelmingly in your favor. What that menu might be changes from night to night, from season to season, and with Chef David Punch's whim. ❖ I'd like to say you're the one for me, but I'm not into restaurant monogamy. I wish there were more out there like you, though. And maybe soon there will be. Word is, owner Krista Kranyak is opening a similar restaurant across the river. Will you still see me if I start something with your younger sibling?

# HUNGRY MOTHER

★★★⯪

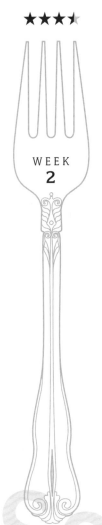

*233 Cardinal Medeiros Ave., Cambridge*
*617-499-0090*
*www.hungrymothercambridge.com*
*Major credit cards accepted. Some stairs,*
*but wheelchairs can be accommodated.*

**PRICES** *Snacks: $3-$4. Appetizers: $7-$13.*
*Entrees: $16-$25. Desserts: $6-$7.*

**HOURS** *Tue-Sun dinner 5-10 p.m., bar and*
*snacks till 1 a.m.*

**NOISE LEVEL** *Convivial.*

## • MAY WE SUGGEST •

Shrimp and grits; French-style gnocchi;
cornmeal catfish.

TASTING NOTES

**BOSTON • CAMBRIDGE**

**WHEN RACHEL MILLER MUNZER** and Alon Munzer ran Rachel's Kitchen in Bay Village, they turned the postage stamp-size sandwich shop into a cornerstone of the neighborhood. They did it by serving great sandwiches, but also by making everyone feel at home. ❖ Now they've partnered with chef Barry Maiden and former Sel de la Terre manager John Kessen to open Hungry Mother, a not-quite-as-small marvel of a restaurant that expertly brings together Southern dishes and French technique. The restaurant is refined, in a hip, vintage-jacket-and-mint-julep way, but it's also comfortable. The hosts still make everyone feel at home. ❖ Maiden's food, too, is refined yet comfortable. He's cooked at L'Espalier, Sel de la Terre, and Lumiere, and the man knows his way around a vichyssoise: pure, creamy, luxurious, with layers of flavor. But he's from Virginia — the restaurant is named for a state park there — and that's where the small menu's heart lies, a salute to peanuts and sorghum, cornmeal and grits. ❖ Even the simplest of dishes display a mastery of technique. Anything in a cornmeal batter — oysters, green tomatoes, catfish — is a beautiful thing, crisp and greaseless. Roasted chicken is juicy, something any bistro table would be honored to present, though here it's served with jalapeno-green garlic spoon bread, beet greens, and red-eye gravy "jus" — tres down home. ❖ Shrimp and grits — elevated comforted food, made with the gold standard Anson Mills grits and tiny shrimp that melt in your mouth — includes house-made tasso ham and ramps. A departure from the rest of the menu, French-style gnocchi practically float out of the bowl and into your mouth — they are more like savory little pastries than dumplings. ❖ A mint julep, a.k.a. the No. 3, is made with sorghum. The house cocktails go by numbers — the No. 1 (rye, Dr. Pepper, and bitters) and the No. 10 (bourbon, sweet tea, and limoncello) are standouts. ❖ Much attention has been paid to the beverages. There's a very good beer selection, and the wine list, like the food, is affordable. It includes quite a few Burgundies, Bordeaux, and other French selections, as well as some New World options; it's a diverse, interesting range. ❖ For dessert, buttermilk pie is a dense, custard-like confection in a graham cracker crust; it goes down easy, not too sweet, not too tangy. Old-fashioned chocolate cake is a giant layered slab that will make any chocolate cake fan happy, particularly served with a cold glass of Thatcher Farm milk. ❖ The Hungry Mother team understands hospitality as well as food. They've created a restaurant that feels both homey and happening.

D.F.

# RADIUS

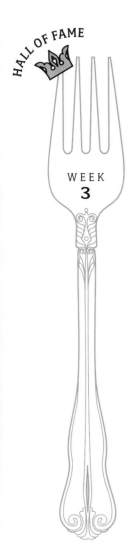

WEEK
**3**

*8 High St., Boston (Financial District)*
*617-426-1234*
*www.radiusrestaurant.com*
*MasterCard, Visa, American Express accepted.*
*Fully accessible.*

**PRICES** *Lunch: first courses $10-$17, main courses $19-$26. Dinner: first courses $15-$25, main courses $32-$46, tasting menus $75-$135. Desserts: $8-$14.*

**HOURS** *Lunch: Mon-Fri 11:30 a.m.-2:30 p.m. Dinner: Mon-Thu 5:30-10 p.m., Fri-Sat 5:30-11 p.m.*

**NOISE LEVEL** *Conversation possible.*

## MAY WE SUGGEST

Foie gras a la Radius; slow-roasted prime rib eye with Robuchon potatoes and red wine sauce; Cinema Paradiso (for two) with caramel popcorn, slushy, chocolate-covered raisins.

TASTING NOTES
_____
_____
_____
_____
_____

**WHAT MAKES AN** experience worth the tab? Radius, one of those at the pinnacle of Boston dining, opened to fanfare in 1998. It immediately became a destination as its chef and co-owner, Michael Schlow, gained national recognition. A decade later, the mature Radius still flies high. ❖ There's an ambience of luxury — heavy table linens, soft lighting, sound-proofing, leather-bound menus. The waitstaff obviously prides itself on professionalism — quick, helpful, unobtrusive, and for the most part, very efficient. The wine list is pricey, but boasts intelligent choices. ❖ The chefs create delicious theater on the plate. On a summer menu, a crab and zucchini appetizer evolves down a rectangular dish: there's molded crab salad slightly tangy with lime juice, two delicately fried zucchini blossoms, and small soft-shell crabs crisply fried but without oiliness. A drizzle of zucchini sauce and tiny zucchini slices march down either side of the plate. ❖ Schlow was always known for his brawny approach to flavors. Now the main courses are more nuanced, showing off their virtues in layers rather than in one punch. Sometimes, many components add up to the final palette. A thick cut of black sea bass, its skin crisp and flesh creamy, sits in the middle of a rimmed plate. Around it are braised morels, little chunks of rock shrimp, and swirls of dark-green arugula pistou, a French version of pesto. Then the waiter pours in a shallow puddle of fragrant mushroom consomme. The result is multifaceted — the taste and texture of the fish, the bright taste of the pistou, the sweetness of the shrimp all distinct but melded. ❖ Along with edgy, modern elements such as foam emulsions on some dishes, there are dressed-up comfort dishes including a perfectly crisped roast chicken or a hefty slow-roasted rib-eye steak with creamy, cheesy potatoes. ❖ Desserts can range from elaborate extravaganzas — the Cinema Paradiso for two features caramel corn in a box, popcorn-flavored ice cream, a slushy, and chocolate candy — to a refreshing set of sorbets. That sweet but spiky ending accents Radius's raison d'etre. It's expensive, yes, but full of culinary revelations and consistent service. A dinner at Radius is a rare luxury for most of us. But a worthy one.

ALISON ARNETT, *Globe Correspondent*

# SORELLINA

WEEK
**4**

*1 Huntington Ave., Boston (Back Bay)*

*617-412-4600*

*www.sorellinaboston.com*

*All major cards accepted. Fully accessible.*

**PRICES** *First courses: $13-$24. Pasta: $13-$29. Second courses: $32-$85. Desserts: $8-$12.*

**HOURS** *Sun-Thu 5:30-10 p.m., Fri-Sat 5:30-11 p.m.*

**NOISE LEVEL** *Plenty of padding and soundproofing means conversation is fairly easy.*

## MAY WE SUGGEST

Yellowtail crudo with crushed cherry peppers and citrus; pork chop with Tuscan beans and dried-fruit mostarda; mocha-meringue chocolate semifreddo.

TASTING NOTES

**FOR A PERFECT** example of the shifting landscape of local restaurants, just walk into Sorellina in Back Bay, where tables are crowded with well-dressed men and women blithely chatting as they carve into veal Milanese and steaks at $40 or more while downing oversized martinis. Owned by a team led by chef Jamie Mammano of Mistral and Teatro, Sorellina is Italian luxe, full of voluptuously rich tastes and textures. With its fairly pricey wine list and careful, pleasant service, Sorellina is high-end dining without the formality of fancy-occasion restaurants. ❖ The lush yet understated design of whites streaked with umber browns, and the texture and padding that make the room fairly quiet create a soothing and comfortable ambience. ❖ Sorellina isn't out to shock or even surprise you with its food. One evening we start with yellowtail crudo, the Italian version of sashimi, its clean flesh made slightly astringent by orange and lemon and by tiny jolts of crushed cherry peppers. Green beans, dressed up with a sprightly vinaigrette, are offset by the sweet crunch of sunchokes and the lemony notes of artichokes. This is an Italian restaurant with very little pasta, a trend that these days signals that the restaurant is expensive. That's evidenced by American Kobe beef fashioned into big meatballs and served with long, thin tubes of macaroni in a rich wine sauce. ❖ Main courses are generously proportioned, and in steakhouse style, vegetables are offered at a separate price on the side. Veal Milanese covers the large plate with its golden, crumbed surface, and is flanked by a small pile of shaved endive. The veal is perfectly moist under its crumbs and gets a lift from the sharpness of a sherry vinaigrette. A special of swordfish is delicate and moist, with a wonderful braised celery topping. A whole yellowtail snapper roasted at a very high temperature has a lovely crackly skin protecting its delicate flesh. It takes a little negotiating around the bones to eat a fish this way, but the reward is a clean, natural taste. ❖ Desserts follow the same decadent path with an excellent tiramisu, and a mocha-meringue semifreddo as irresistible as a highly flavored cloud. ❖ Sorellina's food is almost uniformly wonderful, and for that and the excellent service, the very high prices don't seem out of line. The sense of daring that other chefs and other restaurants can impart in their food can be lacking here. Yet, for a fine meal and a coddled experience, Sorellina is a sure bet.

# LA VOILE

★★⯪☆

WEEK
**5**

*261 Newbury St., Boston (Back Bay)*
*617-587-4200*
*www.lavoileboston.net*
*Major credit cards accepted.*
*Wheelchair accessible.*

**PRICES** *Appetizers: $9-$27. Entrees: $18-$44. Desserts: $7-$9.*

**HOURS** *Lunch: Mon-Sat noon-2:30 p.m., Sun noon-3 p.m. Dinner: Mon-Sat 5:30-10:30 p.m., Sun 5:30-9:30 p.m.*

**NOISE LEVEL** *Conversation easy.*

## MAY WE SUGGEST

Fish soup; bone marrow; mussels in a cream broth; roasted free-range chicken; veal sweetbreads; prunes in Armagnac, financier, and cinnamon ice cream; cheese.

TASTING NOTES

_____
_____
_____
_____
_____

**CANNES IS KNOWN FOR** its film festival, its beaches and balmy climate, its glamour and the matching price tag. It's not particularly known for its food. ❖ Newbury Street is significantly less beachy, but it has its own brand of glamour, and its matching price tag. It also is not particularly known for its food. ❖ But it now Newbury Street has one up on Cannes. The brasserie La Voile ("the sail") relocated from the French city, where it was called La Voile au Vent. The owners, enticed by an American sailor friend, packed up many of the recipes and some of the decor and moved everything here. ❖ As soon as the restaurant opened, people took notice, raving about delicious dishes and reasonable prices. The place was busy every night. Word was out: There's real French food on Newbury Street. ❖ You will eat richly here, in a room filled with dark wood, mirrors, and nautical touches: photographs of boats, model ships, French verse about the ocean painted on the walls. Staff members sweep in with appetizers — ravioli, fish soup, foie gras creme brulee — and the man delivering a plate of monolithic bones filled with marrow sets it down with a chuckle. "Enjoy your cholesterol," he says, then relents. "No, no, it's good fat." ❖ Good fat indeed. The flavor is clean, like a gentle beef broth, not at all gamey. The ravioli are tiny, filled with cheese and topped with a swoosh of pesto; in the thinnest of cream sauces, they are rich but surprisingly light. ❖ The fish soup is heady with intense seafood flavor, slightly warm in the mouth without being truly spicy. Traditional toasts, shredded cheese, and garlicky rouille are served alongside, but even without them, each bite tastes as good as the last. In an entrée of sweetbreads, velvety offal is poached and then braised in cream sauce with a generous serving of morels. The sauce is ridiculously rich and satisfying, and the sweetbreads melt in the mouth, but it's the morels that put the dish over the top. ❖ Roasted chicken is prepared simply, using the recipe from Paris restaurant L'Ami Louis (famed for its roast chicken) — a free-range bird, a few herbs, crispy skin, juicy meat. Just what you want from roast chicken, with a little cocotte of creamy mashed potatoes alongside. ❖ Finish with cheese or a cake topped with Armagnac-soaked prunes and cinnamon ice cream and toast to a Newbury Street restaurant worth getting excited about.

D.F.

# LOCKE-OBER

HALL OF FAME

WEEK
6

3 Winter Place, Boston (Downtown)
617-542-1340
www.lockeober.com
Visa, MasterCard, American Express,
Diners accepted. One step at entrance,
one at dining room.

**PRICES** Lunch: three-course prix fixe $25,
soup and oyster bar $8-$19. Dinner:
appetizers $8-$22, oyster bar $11-$42,
entrees $25-$62, desserts $6-$12.

**HOURS** Lunch: Mon-Fri 11:30 a.m.-2:30 p.m.
Dinner: Mon-Thu 5:30-10 p.m.,
Fri-Sat 5:30-11 p.m.

**NOISE LEVEL** Plenty of padding and
upholstery keeps noise down.

## MAY WE SUGGEST

JFK's lobster bisque; venison loin with
gnocchi; baked Alaska.

TASTING NOTES
_____
_____
_____
_____
_____

WE TEND TO THINK of Locke-Ober, with its long and storied history, as serving traditional New England fare. But under Lydia Shire, who took over the restaurant in 2001, the menu has become more and more baroque, with dishes that match the magnificence of the room. Shire carefully resurrected favorites from the old menu — lobster Savannah, JFK's lobster stew, calves liver, oysters and filet mignon among them. Some entrees are as ornate as the heavy silver warming dishes that line the mahogany bar along the side of the dining room. Others are simple but strong. ❖ Venison loin imparts a pronounced smoky flavor and herbal bursts of rosemary along with currants and vinegary-laced fruits. With the hefty portion of meat comes a row of tender little pillows of gnocchi dusted with white truffle powder, so fragrant you want to bury your nose in them. The voluptuousness of the meats contrasts with the simplicity of halibut, beautifully snowy and cooked perfectly, dressed with a tangy confit of Meyer lemon and a sprinkling of crisped capers. Desserts range from the traditional homey, such as Indian pudding, to the spectacular, such as baked Alaska. ❖ As much as the food, the dining room with its burnished wood and deep armchairs evokes a dining heritage almost past. Locke-Ober is one of the few places in Boston that still at least makes an attempt at a dress code; a notice on the website suggests jackets for men, though the code doesn't seem to be enforced. And the courtly demeanor of some of the waiters as they place a platter of oysters in front of a patron or lift a silver cover from a plate bespeaks decades of service. ❖ Dining at Locke-Ober is still an event, and with a long but pricey wine list and substantial entree prices, it's not a casual night out for most of us. But on a weekday, the room is quiet and the waitstaff, though competent and quick, seems rather disinterested. The cooking, along with Shire's inspiration, is truly exciting. Let's hope the dining room staff can keep pace.

A.A.

# NEPTUNE OYSTER

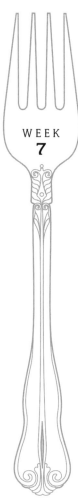

63 Salem St., Boston (North End)

617-742-3474

www.neptuneoyster.com

All major cards accepted. Two steps up.

**PRICES** Appetizers: $11-$14; oysters $2-$2.80, plateau di mare $48-$85. Salads: $14-$16. Sandwiches: $13-$25. Entrees: $23-$34.

**HOURS** Sun-Thu 11:30 a.m.-11 p.m., Fri-Sat 11:30 a.m.-midnight. Reservations for large parties only.

**NOISE LEVEL** Small space with hard surfaces; noisy on busy nights.

## MAY WE SUGGEST

Oysters, any variety from the nightly list; lobster roll; North End cioppino with grilled fish and shellfish.

TASTING NOTES

WEEK
7

**T**HE NARROW STREETS of the North End are crammed with eateries, one after another along Salem and Hanover streets. Amid this profusion, Neptune Oyster stands out. So tiny that diners along the 26 banquette seats and the 16 bar stools sit nearly literally cheek-to-cheek, Neptune has the congenial ambience of a house party. ❖ The look of the place, old but new with a marble-topped bar, tin ceilings, and a minimalist aesthetic, gives it a cool vibe. Regular customers, many of whom live in the tight neighborhoods near the restaurant, tend to recommend favorite dishes to newcomers as they chat with the bartender or watch a young woman shucking oysters in the window visible from the street. And the wide selection of wines, many by the glass, adds to the enjoyment of the place. ❖ Oysters are the biggest draw with up to 12 varieties, listed by origin, offered on a big board. There are other dishes, too, such as a great lobster roll (available hot with butter or cold with mayo) and a delicious salmon filet with bits of crispy duck confit and pea tendrils plus rotating daily specials. Neptune's menu is short, but intelligently chosen — a beautifully made mussel salad with julienned fennel and a light, tangy dressing studded with pistachios; the red snapper entree, perfectly cooked, with big, cracked green olives and nuggets of roasted garlic; that fantastic lobster roll, bursting with flavor; sardines fashioned into an unusual sandwich. ❖ Jeff Nace and his wife, Kelli, opened Neptune Oyster in 2004. He had worked for years at Olives and other Todd English restaurants, and he knew he wanted a restaurant with an Old World feel concentrating on New England seafood. Although many dishes have an Italian slant, this cuisine is much more eclectic, and includes a few meat entrees such as beef tenderloin and burgers. ❖ There are some detrimental points in what is a smashing little restaurant. A green salad or two would help offset all the fish. Espresso would be nice, but you have to respect North End restaurateurs for skipping coffee and desserts and sending patrons off to the neighborhood coffee shops. And though noise is understand-able with the restaurant's pretty tiled floors and hard surfaces, turning down the music would lessen the clamor. ❖ Still, Neptune is well worth seeking out. It gleams like a pearl.

# TAMARIND BAY

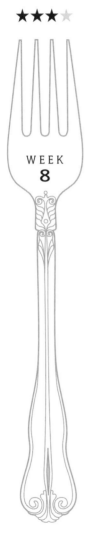

★★★☆

*75 Winthrop St., Cambridge (Harvard Square)*
*617-491-4552*
*www.tamarind-bay.com*
*MasterCard, Visa, American Express,*
*Discover accepted. Short flight of stairs*
*to entrance.*

**PRICES** *Lunch: buffet $8.95-$9.95.*
*Dinner: appetizers $4.50-$8.50,*
*entrees $9.50-$20.50, breads $3-$3.50,*
*desserts $4.50-$6.50.*

**HOURS** *Lunch: Mon-Fri noon-2:30 p.m.,*
*Sat-Sun noon-3 p.m. Dinner: nightly*
*5-10:30 p.m.*

**NOISE LEVEL** *Tightly-spaced room and low*
*ceiling mean noise if room is crowded.*

WEEK
**8**

## MAY WE SUGGEST

Paneer marinated in coriander and
spices; rogan josh with goat; mahi mahi
in carom seed sauce; garlic nan.

TASTING NOTES
_____
_____
_____
_____
_____

 18

**WE THINK WE KNOW** Indian food. We've eaten curries and dal, dabbled in mint chutneys, and enjoyed basketfuls of nan and poori. We've figured out that dosas, those paper-thin crepes, are from the southern part of the country, and moghul sauces are modeled after dishes from the royal courts. We realize that tandoori grilled meats and fish come with slices of lemon and maybe some sliced onion. ❖ We're confident we know Indian, at least until the first bite of Tamarind Bay's bhuna paneer, a firm, mild cheese marinated in coriander and spices and then grilled. The cheese is pale golden with saffron, the spices lively on the tongue, the finely chopped coriander bright green and fresh. The grilling gives the homemade cheese a smoky edge. It's nothing like the pale, flaccid paneer that often is only a sponge for other flavors. This paneer has character. ❖ Rogan josh, a staple on Indian menus, here gets an extra depth of flavor by being made of goat, not lamb, as it probably would be in India, one of the owners tells me in a later phone conversation. I can tell when I'm eating the goat that the deep red and rather oily sauce brims with spices, yet the flavor is intense but not fiery. Even a dish of chicken, first grilled in the tandoor and then served in a creamy tomato sauce, is so subtly flavorful that it's a revelation. ❖ Vik Kapoor, one of the owners, says the intent was to showcase what Indian food can be, focusing on modern Indian cooking. As is true at most Indian restaurants, vegetarians can find a range of dishes. Some, like a mix of mushrooms, fresh green peas, and onions in a tomato masala, subtly show off seasonal virtues, while others, like a soupy casserole of black lentils, have earthier, more sustaining tastes. Mahi mahi done in a curry-like yellow gravy flavored with carom seeds is a little well done, but carom (also called ajwain) sauce, with a golden color and a pungent, almost pickle-like flavor, is fantastic. ❖ Only a few desserts are offered — coconut rice pudding and thread-like rice noodles in custard are both sweet and pleasant enough — and service in general can be harried, sometimes even chaotic. That's probably to be expected in the tight, basement-level space this restaurant occupies in Harvard Square. ❖ Eating at Tamarind Bay is an adventure, and mostly a delightful one. For Indian food this enticing, it's worth a little forbearance.

# STELLA

★★✦☆

*1525 Washington St., Boston (South End)*
*617-247-7747*
*www.bostonstella.com*
*All major cards accepted. Fully accessible.*

**PRICES** *Antipasti: $8-$12.*
*Pizza, pasta: $15-$19. Entrees: $18-$30.*
*Desserts: $6-$8.*

**HOURS** *Nightly 5:30-11 p.m., bar menu until 1:30 a.m.*

**NOISE LEVEL** *Can be very noisy.*

## ⊙ MAY WE SUGGEST ⊙

Crudo misto; tagliatelle Bolognese;
Sicilian swordfish.

TASTING NOTES

WEEK
9

**IT WAS A STEAMY** late-June evening and Stella pulsed with people. They crowded the bar area and surged into the dining room, mobbing the hostess as they inquired about tables. Waiters and waitresses hurried steaming bowls of pasta with Bolognese and fancifully topped pizzas to waiting diners. Outside, the laughter of those on the terrace caused pedestrians a block away to turn and stare at the restaurant's lights. Stella was hopping. Several years later, it still is.

❖ Owner Evan Deluty has said he wanted a neighborhood restaurant where customers could come several nights a week. There are good reasons for Stella's success, the most notable being the look of the place. Stella has gorgeous bones: Long windows and high ceilings let light in. The white-on-white palette makes the place feel even airier, and the minimalist molded white chairs, high-tech nylon weave flooring and marble tables add to the clean lines. ❖ Stella's pricing, with most entrees kept under $25, adds to its popularity. The menu is made up of offerings that might be called Italian lite and the food can range from all right to really fine. Crudo misto, the Italian version of sashimi, consists of pristine curls of tuna and salmon under a tart limoncello vinaigrette with a salt-sprinkled bread stick to offset the citrus flavors. The Bolognese sauce over tagliatelle has a meaty depth, but still is light enough not to sink like a stone. Grilled pizzas seem to be the crowd-pleasers. A pizza with three kinds of mushrooms and white truffle oil is topped with plenty of funghi, arugula, and cheese: so much so that the topping overwhelms the crust and makes it soggy. A simpler pepperoni version with a judicious amount of ingredients is much better. ❖ Simplicity reigns in the main courses, which is great if the cooking is on target, but not if meats or fish are overcooked. Stella's rib eye is juicy and flavorful, and tuna arrabiatta (angry style) offsets a peppery, garlicky coating with a slightly sweet caponata. Swordfish Siciliano has the same mix of sweet-tart accompaniments to the strong-flavored fish. ❖ Desserts aren't Stella's strong points. Cannoli are filled with thick, stiff cream, sticky and sweet. The best is a coffee mousse, light and airy with crushed almond biscotti as a counterpoint. But to fit in among the beautiful at Stella, dessert might be too much, anyway. On many nights, the place can be the epicenter of cool, and if you choose wisely, you can even eat well.

# O YA

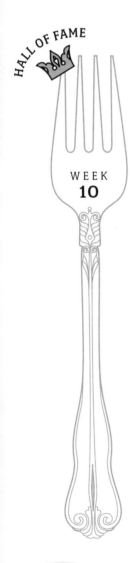

WEEK
**10**

9 East St., Boston (Leather District)
617-654-9900
www.oyarestaurantboston.com
Major credit cards accepted.
Wheelchair accessible.

**PRICES** Small plates: $8-$58.
(Wagyu steak, $189.99.)

**HOURS** Tue-Thu 5-9:30 p.m., Fri-Sat 5-10 p.m.

**NOISE LEVEL** Conversation easy.

## MAY WE SUGGEST

Kinmedai sashimi; foie gras nigiri; onsen
egg; clam chowder; chicken yakitori;
soy milk blancmange; warm chocolate
pudding cake.

TASTING NOTES

_____
_____
_____
_____
_____

**BOSTON MAY BE** one of the few remaining cities that doesn't have an outpost of Nobu. And that's just as well if it leaves more room for independent restaurants like o ya. ❖ Opened in 2007 on a little side street near South Station, o ya feels like a speakeasy, looks like a spread in a design magazine, and serves as a temple to perfect, pricey sashimi and sushi. (It also happens to have a chef and co-owner, Tim Cushman, who apprenticed with the eponymous Nobu Matsuhisa.) The restaurant occupies an unobtrusive brick building, its entrance so hidden that it feels as if a secret knock or password might grant access to a stash of illegal hooch. But there's no hooch here. (There is a sake sommelier, though.) And the door swings open unhindered; beyond it, a gravel-lined path leads to a room with brick walls, wood beams, and shoji-covered windows. It conveys Japanese inn and New England warehouse. ❖ The place seats around 40, and eating here feels like being one of the chosen few. The offerings are so precisely composed they seem as much like art as they do food. A sweet Kumamoto oyster adorned with pearls of watermelon is served in a mini bamboo steamer filled with ice; three slices of the buttery, coral-skinned fish called kinmedai are set on a plate, their edges curled under just so. Most dishes at o ya are about four bites, and with a few changes from night to night, the menu encompasses roughly 70 of them, plus five desserts and nearly 20 kinds of sake. ❖ Here comes a serving of wild bluefin toro tartare that melts on the tongue. Now a bowl of clam chowder, a tour-de-force version enlivened by crunchy tempura bits. One dish holds braised pork served with toothsome "Boston baked" rice beans and soy-maple sauce, a sweet-salty wink at local tradition. Then a plate of yakitori, some of the best we've had, and an onsen egg poached low and slow, floating in dashi. ❖ The list goes on and most of the dishes even warrant the price tag. The foie gras nigiri, for example, is one flawless bite of creamy, crisp-edged richness, set in bold face by a chaser of aged sake. For dessert there's soy milk blancmange, a pot de creme-like concoction, its creaminess set off by the woody flavors of Thai tea and crunchy, tapioca-esque basil seeds; or warm chocolate pudding cake, divested of hoariness by the presence of cherries in shiso simple syrup. ❖ So who needs Nobu?

# TORO

WEEK
**11**

*1704 Washington St., Boston (South End)*
*617-536-4300*
*www.toro-restaurant.com*
*All major cards accepted. Fully accessible.*

**PRICES** *Pinchos: $4-$10.*
*Tapas, small plates: $5-$16.*
*Dishes for 2-4: $26-$38. Cheeses: $17-$27.*
*Desserts: $7.*

**HOURS** *Sun-Wed 5:30-10:15 p.m.,*
*Thu-Sat 5:30 p.m.-12:45 a.m. No reservations.*

**NOISE LEVEL** *Deafening when busy, which*
*is most of the time.*

## MAY WE SUGGEST

Croquetas de bacalao (salt cod fritters);
mejillas de ternera con Rioja (veal cheeks
with prunes and Rioja); paella Valencia;
churros with chocolate.

TASTING NOTES

**T**HE SPANISH TAPAS restaurant created by chef Ken Oringer in 2005 still causes a stir. Toro is wildly popular, insanely crowded, and ridiculously noisy. Chatterers on Internet message boards still complain about the service. The waits are routinely so long that would-be customers give up and wander across the street to other establishments. And once inside, waits for a table and for food to be delivered can be brutal. ❖ True, the room, with its long bar, a chalkboard listing tapas in loopy longhand, and high-topped communal tables running down the center, is cleverly done in a minimalist warehouse style. True, the pulsating crowd is beautiful; the waiters are enthusiastic about the food and the chefs energetically rush about in the open kitchen. And when you get to the food — tender veal cheeks braised in Rioja wine with Armagnac-laced prunes melting away in their pretty little Staub casserole; amazingly light and tender salt cod croquettes with a puff of mayonnaise and preserved lemon rings; crispy roasted and generously salted Brussels sprouts — it can make the aggravations of the place slide away. ❖ The tapas can be tiny: a little potato and onion omelet with aioli, a dish of chickpeas with bits of chorizo and very little spinach, roasted eggplant bright with vinegary flavor, a little clay pot of wild mushrooms sauteed in garlic and olive oil and topped with an egg, its white whipped into foam. Tapas of flavorful shrimp in garlic are reminiscent of Barcelona. And the made-to-order paella, a big copper pan brimming with shrimp, clams, mussels, pieces of chicken, a scattering of peas, and fantastic, slightly crusty saffron rice, can draw sighs of satisfaction for its richly classic flavors. ❖ Not everything is traditional. It's hard to imagine a Spanish tapas joint serving plump little burgers on miniature buns with zigzags of house-made catsup. But they're delicious. Ditto for the grilled ears of corn covered with bits of cheese, served in every season but irresistible, nonetheless. And it's hard to go wrong with crisp churros (like long crullers) and deeply intense hot chocolate to finish a meal. ❖ Toro's teasingly lovely flavors and the ever-changing menu are alluring. But you'll have to plan to satisfy the urge for Toro's tapas. A leisurely dinner or one on the spur of the moment is unlikely; best to either get there very early (before 6 p.m.) or be prepared to be patient and people-watch while you wait. Even after several years in business, Toro is still almost too hot to handle.

# BANQ

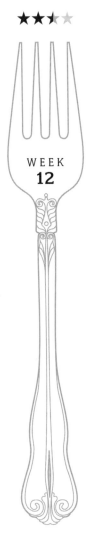

★★★⯪☆

1375 Washington St., Boston (South End)
617-451-0077
www.banqrestaurant.com
Major credit cards accepted.
Wheelchair accessible.

**PRICES** *Asian Amusé: $4.50-$6.
Appetizers: $9-$15. Entrees: $19-$26.
Desserts: $9-$10.*

**HOURS** *Mon-Sat 5:30 p.m.-1 a.m.
Sun 5:30-11 p.m.
Brunch Sat-Sun 11 a.m.-2:30 p.m.*

**NOISE LEVEL** *Can be very loud.*

WEEK
12

## MAY WE SUGGEST

Soy ginger lamb spring roll; fire-charred
bay scallop with Indian lentils; baby
beets; flash-seared Vietnamese shrimp
with glass noodles; grilled cod.

TASTING NOTES

**THE MAIN DRAW** at Banq may be the ribs. They're made of blond wood, so don't try to eat them. Cut into organic curves, they are affixed to the walls and ceilings to form an undulating interior landscape. It's very cool — distractingly so. Banq's interior seems as much of an attraction as its Asian-influenced French food. ❖ The menu's descriptions make the mouth water, full of intriguing ingredients and combinations: Soy ginger lamb spring roll with Roquefort glaze. Fire-charred sirloin with smoked cha choy, cilantro and taro pave, caramelized lotus seed, creamy chanterelle sauce. ❖ But as vivid as these dishes sound, in practice they are often muted. France does the talking while India, Japan, and Thailand whisper in its ear. Much of Banq's food is delicious. If you're expecting to be smacked around by chili lime green beans and smoked Darjeeling tea jus, however, it's disappointing when your taste buds mainly encounter the polite Cornish hen breasts they accompany. ❖ The menu is divided into three sections: Asian Amusé, appetizers, and entrees. ❖ The first category consists of small tastes to wake the palate. The soy ginger lamb spring rolls are crisp parcels that give way in shards to the gaminess of lamb, then the gaminess of Roquefort, the sheep-milk blue a subtle highlight. A nicely cooked, creamy scallop is paired with earthy, Indian-spiced lentils. (Chef Ranveer Brar was previously at the Claridges hotel in New Delhi.) Baby beets, glowing pink, are made sweet with mirin and served with a little round of tangy, smooth chevre. ❖ A Vietnamese shrimp appetizer is perhaps the most purely Asian dish in the house. Shrimp are dipped in crumbs and seared, then served with spicy glass noodles fragrant with lemongrass, kaffir lime, and galangal. ❖ Entrees move further away from the Asian and hew closer to the French. With one diner's first bite of grilled cod with papadum and onion crust, Pommery banana flower relish, lotus root Provencal, and green tea miso beurre blanc, for example, he simply says, "Yum, butter!" And it is yummy, nicely cooked, with a pleasant crunch on the exterior. But where's the green tea, the miso, the banana flower relish? The dish, as good as it is, tantalizes with a complexity it doesn't deliver. ❖ Banq looks and sounds exotic, but it tastes classic. There's nothing inherently wrong with that. Still, if all those enticing flavors would only speak a little louder, the food would stand a better chance of commanding our attention.

D.F.

# RIALTO

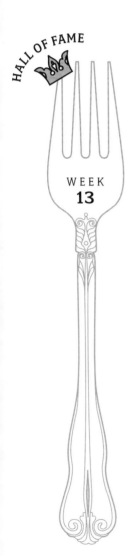

HALL OF FAME

WEEK
**13**

*1 Bennett St., Charles Hotel,*
*Cambridge (Harvard Square)*
*617-661-5050*
*www.rialto-restaurant.com*
*All major cards accepted.*
*Wheelchair accessible.*

**PRICES** *First courses: $9-$16.*
*Second courses: $11-$18.*
*Main courses: $17-$43. Desserts: $9-$21.*

**HOURS** *Dinner: Mon-Fri 5:30-10 p.m.,*
*Sat 5:30-11 p.m., Sun 5:30-9 p.m.*

**NOISE LEVEL** *Conversation is possible*
*even when the room is busy.*

## MAY WE SUGGEST

Tuna crudo with beets and blood
orange; red wine risotto with radicchio
and almond pesto; slow-braised rabbit
with olives, figs, and chestnuts; espresso
and orange semifreddo.

TASTING NOTES

**RIALTO IS NOW** a solo act. Jody Adams, a chef whose generous and natural cooking has delighted diners for many years, took over this restaurant in 2007 and is making it her own. ❖ Adams revamped her Mediterranean menu, creating one that's all Italian, except for a small selection of old favorites. The expansive wine list offers Italian vintages by regions, as well as other selections. ❖ Adams also brightened the dining room that overlooks Harvard Square, with subtle changes such as white shutters instead of black along the long windows; gauzy, wheat-colored curtains that define spaces; and a hostess desk at the entrance to help orient diners. The colors are soothing, and the dining room is significantly quieter than it used to be. ❖ What always makes Adams so delightful as a chef is the ability to think through her food, beyond techniques or styles, to the essence. When she says she's after simplicity, that doesn't mean too plain. But it does mean that, in most dishes, the flavors will be clear and the finish clean. Take a dish of spinach gnocchi with spring vegetables, beautifully light and finished with a rich cream sauce imbued with Parmesan and dotted with fava beans, peas, and herbs. Rialto's red wine risotto is so memorable that it outshines excellent versions tasted in Rome. It's a humble-looking dish, a sort of muted shade of beigey-brown flecked with wine-shaded radicchio. But its mild flavor offset with the sharp kick of radicchio and a slightly crunchy almond pesto is addictive. ❖ Although fish dishes are fine, it's the meat dishes that shine on a spring menu. Slow-braised rabbit is especially flavorful and tender in its lovely dark pan sauce. Guinea hen, a rarity on menus, is another great dish, its skin crackly and flesh soft. A little potato and tomato tart, though, is very simple and almost overshadows the bird. And Adams's famous slow-roasted duck is enough reason to head for the classics section of the menu. ❖ Not everything works as well, with a few dishes too bland or undersalted. And the service can vary, especially in the rather dim back room. But when it's on, this is a wonderful place to linger over dessert — from a simple buttermilk sorbet with blueberries to a rich espresso and orange semifreddo. ❖ By concentrating on one cuisine, Adams risked having her restaurant be submerged by a sea of Italian eateries. Yet the new Rialto proved that a great chef can plumb the depths of cuisine and envelope the diner in her excitement.

A.A.

# RENDEZVOUS

★★★☆

WEEK
**14**

*502 Mass. Ave., Cambridge (Central Square)*
*617-576-1900*
*www.rendezvouscentralsquare.com*
*MasterCard, Visa, American Express accepted.*
*Fully accessible.*

**PRICES** *Appetizers: $8-$14.*
*Entrees: $20-$26. Desserts $7-$8.*
*Sunday 3-course prix fixe: $38.*

**HOURS** *Sun-Thu 5-10 p.m., Fri-Sat 5-11 p.m.*

**NOISE LEVEL** *Soundproofing helps but it can be noisy.*

## ◦ MAY WE SUGGEST ◦

Vegetable antipasto with roasted eggplant puree; Gascon-style duck three ways; warm chocolate cake with hazelnut pralines.

TASTING NOTES

_____
_____
_____
_____

**YOU'D THINK** that discovering a restaurant you really like would be the best part of reviewing. But there comes a sad point when the eating part is over and one can't look forward to returning for another taste. All those joys of being a regular are denied by the requirements of chasing after the next new place. Luckily, others can be Rendezvous regulars. ❖ One wants to be able to savor again and again the tiny, light gnocchi suspended over a hearty ragout of braised oxtail and sprinkled with shavings of tangy piave cheese. The same goes for the heady, fragrant garlic soup or the duck three ways, with its meaty sausage, silken confit, and flavorful rare-cooked breast meat. ❖ Steve Johnson, who made his name in Boston at Hamersley's and the Blue Room, opened Rendezvous in 2005. The restaurant, a transformed old Burger King, has a crisp, spare look, with lots of masculine browns and woods with mustards and orange for accents. The bar at the front has a long, low table so that diners can comfortably eat there. ❖ Johnson's food sensibility shines in Rendezvous. The style is a little bit French with some Moroccan touches, a little bit California with a Mediterranean feel. Mostly, Johnson creates straightforward dishes that taste good. ❖ The menu changes often. Winter might showcase tuna in a vividly flavored tonnato sauce. For summer, the fish entrees could feature striped bass with littlenecks and pesto while meats include a grilled peppered hanger steak or braised rabbit with Spanish ham, chanterelles, and haricots verts. The vegetables in many of these dishes stand out. A vegetable antipasto is beautiful, including sauteed jewel-like carrots with a bit of the leafy top still attached, sweet matchsticks of parsnips, fingerling potatoes, and half a small artichoke covered with a wonderful romescu sauce. Desserts are simple, such as a lemon-buttermilk pudding; the best is a chocolate cake with an elusive undertone of cinnamon and espresso. ❖ Johnson says he spent years looking for the right location for a new place in Cambridge, and that he was determined to have the kind of restaurant that can attract those who live nearby and serve the food he likes at reasonable prices. Rendezvous isn't perfect — the service can be pretty casual and it's sometimes noisy — but Johnson achieves his goal: a restaurant with food you enjoy eating, in a place you enjoy being in.

A.A.

# VINOTECA DI MONICA

WEEK
**15**

*143 Richmond St., Boston (North End)*
*617-227-0311*
*www.monicasonline.com*
*Major credit cards accepted. Wheelchair accessible.*

**PRICES** *Appetizers: $9-$14. Entrees: $18-$32 (specials can run higher). Desserts: $8.*

**HOURS** *Mon-Thu 5-11 p.m., Fri-Sun 5 p.m.-midnight.*

**NOISE LEVEL** *Conversation easy, though the bar side can be a bit noisier.*

## MAY WE SUGGEST

Agnolotti di carne; tajarin with peas and prosciutto; zuppa di pesce.

**TASTING NOTES**

_____

_____

_____

_____

_____

Ital

**WHEN A RESTAURANT** is named after the chefs' mother, it's as sure a sign as any that the place is going to be good. Brothers Jorge, Patrick, and Frank Mendoza-Iturralde christened not one but two restaurants, plus an Italian grocery, after their mother, Monica. The message is clear: These family-run businesses, all in the North End, are labors of love. ❖ Vinoteca di Monica is a revamp of the old Monica's Restaurant, spruced up and with a separate bar area. The main dining room feels warm and welcoming, with deep red walls and comfortable red-and-white striped banquettes. There's a long wine list of bottles from Italy and a menu of unfussy antipasti, salads, pasta dishes, and entrees. Each night there are 10 to 15 specials. ❖ On one evening, the list includes fresh tajarin — long, thin egg noodles — tossed with a little bit of cream sauce, peppered with plentiful shavings of mahogany truffles and parmesan. The dish is both delicate and earthy. In another dish, the same noodles are mixed with peas and crisped prosciutto. ❖ A special of rack of lamb is cooked rare (though ordered medium-rare); the flavor of the lamb, barely salted, stands on its own. It's served with potatoes and sweet roasted garlic, but this dish is really about the meat. Zuppa di pesce is barely zuppa — it's more of a seafood platter — but it does contain an aquarium's worth of pesce. The mussels, lobster, et al. come arrayed on a long plate with a bit of bouillabaisse-like broth at the bottom. ❖ Monica's pasta, tender and fresh, is handmade at the trattoria and sold at Monica's Mercato. Mendoza-Iturralde says he wants to make food that "leaves you with a taste memory," and his pasta succeeds. This is comfort food that avoids being dull. ❖ Dessert offerings include a pleasant creme brulee, rich and thick, with a thin coating of sugar, and a tiramisu that could use a bit more rum. ❖ The menu in the bar is the same as that in the dining room, but the atmosphere is different, fun where the dining room is cozy. This side of the restaurant gets busier as the other starts to empty out. ❖ "We wanted a place where our neighbors and friends could come by, have a drink, watch the game, have a quick bite," Mendoza-Iturralde says. That's just what they've created, and the neighborhood feeling is as pleasing as the pasta.

D.F.

# OLEANA

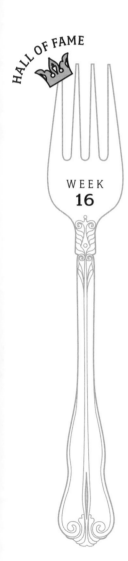

HALL OF FAME

WEEK
16

134 Hampshire St.,
Cambridge (Inman Square)
617-661-0505
www.oleanarestaurant.com
MasterCard, Visa, American Express accepted.
Fully accessible.

**PRICES** *Appetizers: $9-$13.
Entrees: $24-$30. Desserts: $11-$14.*

**HOURS** *Sun-Thu 5:30-10 p.m.,
Fri-Sat 5:30-11 p.m.*

**NOISE LEVEL** *Conversation easy.*

## MAY WE SUGGEST

Armenian bean and walnut pate; fried
mussels and hot peppers with Turkish
tarator sauce; free-range veal and
almond dumpling; baked Alaska.

TASTING NOTES

**WATCHING ANA SORTUN** over the years has been a little like watching a butterfly emerge from her chrysalis. From her beginnings as a chef for the renowned restaurateur Moncef Meddeb, the years at Casablanca, through her quest for her own restaurant (and now a brand new cafe, Sofra), she has shown such resiliency, such curiosity, and such a capacity for hard work that you just had to root for her. ❖ Oleana is the showcase for Sortun's talents and its menu shows the fruits of her interest in Turkish cuisine and the foods of Armenia, Greece, and Portugal. It makes for fascinating eating. Her restaurant is a cozy, Cambridge kind of place, comfortable but the antithesis of slick, with personable service that matches the ambience.

❖ Sortun's food can be a revelation. Before eating Armenian bean and walnut pate, in a category of small plates, you might expect something smooth and rather bland. The taste is a surprise, so much toasty, nutty depth. A Portuguese dish of clams with little chunks of sausage, tomatoes, and potatoes offers an olfactory treat as it comes to the table in its domed copper cooking pan. When the waiter removes the lid, the aroma of the seafood and its broth is almost as delicious as the clams themselves. A dramatic roll of greens encasing a fragrant beef galette, touched with cinnamon, cloves, and other spices, makes more multisensory impressions. ❖ Seasonality is especially important to Oleana's menu since Sortun's husband owns Siena Farms. And her interest in locally grown extends to such products as naturally raised veal. Sortun is also expert at making delicious all those virtuous grains and complex carbohydrates. Her spicy fideos, Spanish toasted vermicelli, with chick peas and Swiss chard, has a nuttiness and a depth of flavor often missing from such vegetarian dishes. Other dishes are straightforward, such as grilled sirloin served on a board with a salad of wilted escarole and a copper pot of Yukon fingerlings in beef broth. Now and then, the spicing can overwhelm the ingredients, but usually even such strong flavors as smoked Spanish paprika or cinnamon and cloves are used judiciously. ❖ Desserts are not to be missed. Pastry chef Maura Kilpatrick creates a spectacular baked Alaska, the elegantly toasted meringue covering layers of crunchy macaroons, coconut ice cream, and passion fruit caramel, as well as other delightful ice cream-based confections. Her fruit tarts and crisps are excellent, too, especially on a summer night in the restaurant's idyllic garden. The casualness of Oleana can make the final tab a little surprising, but the creativity of Sortun and her staff make the experience worth the price.

A.A.

# T.W. FOOD

★★★★

WEEK
**17**

*377 Walden St., Cambridge (Huron Village)*
*617-864-4745*
*www.twfoodrestaurant.com*
*All major cards accepted. Entry wheelchair*
*accessible, bathrooms are not.*

**PRICES** *Appetizers: $4-$19.*
*Entrees: $28-$33. Desserts: $8-$10.*
*Seven-course tasting menus: $69, $95 with*
*wine pairings.*

**HOURS** *Mon-Sat 5-10 p.m., Sun 5-9 p.m.*

**NOISE LEVEL** *Very civilized.*

## MAY WE SUGGEST

Creme brulee of foie gras "for my
mentors"; wild striped bass; "
Scotch & Cigars."

TASTING NOTES

**AT T.W. FOOD** in Cambridge, young husband-and-wife proprietors Tim and Bronwyn Wiechmann are doing something different. It's very much of this region, yet not typical of it. Many of the ingredients are sourced locally — often arriving fresh each day — and thus their flavor is the taste of New England. That is until Tim, the chef, turns them into something else. ❖ As concepts, dishes such as creme brulee of foie gras, chilled heirloom tomato soup with maple-and-sage ice cream, and "Scotch & Cigars" (chocolate mousse with vanilla-tobacco cream and Scotch syrup) seem flown in from California, where restaurants like French Laundry and Manresa flourish. But locally, there is hunger for this kind of cooking — thoughtful, inventive, ingredient-obsessed. ❖ Jamaica Plain's Ten Tables (of which the Wiechmanns are alums) earned a cult following with its comparatively down-to-earth take on the aesthetic. T.W. Food has a more rarefied approach. The dishes are highly crafted, layering the unexpected on the traditional with varying degrees of success. ❖ The menu changes constantly. On one visit, roasted wild striped bass is served with kohlrabi puree, apples, and fish-flavored emulsion. The fish is gleaming white, flaking into glorious, moist hunks. The kohlrabi and the apples feel autumnal for an early August dinner, but the cabbage-y and floral flavors pair well with the fish. Another night, the same fish, just as well cooked, is marinated with kohlrabi, cucumber, and maple syrup, and served with house-cured bacon. The bacon and syrup pairing is intriguing, but the dish doesn't work. Now for the downside of the ever-changing menu: You may never get to eat a certain dish you like again. One thing that is almost always available, however, is the creme brulee of foie gras "for my mentors." (Heads up for the Michelin starry-eyed: The chef apprenticed at Taillevent and L'Arpege.) The custard strikes the perfect balance between liver and creamy sweetness — richness squared, and definitely to be shared. ❖ T.W. Food's wine list, also inclined to change, is sorted by producer and feels both personal and educational. Diners may be bothered by touches that can come off as precious: the many quotation marks on the menus (is the "Wellfleet" oyster not really from Wellfleet?), the servers' insistence on offering "Cambridge filtered" when relaying water choices. But at least those things feel like they come from the heart, and it's hard to fault anyone for caring this much. ❖ If you don't take risks, you don't broaden the culinary landscape. T.W. Food isn't afraid to reach, and for that it gets major points. Long live difference.

D.F.

# BLUE GINGER

WEEK
**18**

583 Washington St., Wellesley
781-283-5790
www.ming.com/blueginger
Major credit cards accepted.
Wheelchair accessible.

**PRICES** Appetizers: $9-$16.
Entrees: $22-$42. Desserts: $12.
Lounge menu: (evenings only) $4-$21.

**HOURS** Lunch: Mon-Fri 11:30 a.m.-2 p.m.
Dinner: Mon-Thu 5:30-9:30 p.m.,
Fri 5:30-10 p.m., Sat 5-10 p.m.

**NOISE LEVEL** Conversation easy.

## MAY WE SUGGEST

Hawaiian bigeye tuna poke; sake-miso
marinated Alaskan butterfish;
Ming's Bings.

TASTING NOTES

**THE MORE** things change, the more they stay the same. Blue Ginger, Ming Tsai's ever-popular Wellesley restaurant, recently turned 10. It marked its birthday with a renovation and expansion, adding a lounge area. ❖ In a review shortly after it opened, the Globe called it "cutting edge," describing such mouthwatering-sounding dishes as foie gras shumai in shallot broth, fish in a marinade of sake and miso, and Indonesian curry pasta with coconut shrimp. These dishes are all still on the menu, but they no longer surprise the way they used to. Asian fusion has become part of the culinary idiom, in part because Tsai put it on TV with shows such as "East Meets West" and "Simply Ming." It's just part of the way we eat. ❖ The foie gras-shiitake shumai still feel fresh. The dumplings come dim sum style in a steamer; to eat them you swish them through a bowl of sauternes-shallot broth, deep brown with caramelized flavors. Neither element quite works on its own, but together they're perfect. Another excellent appetizer is the tuna poke, a crudo inspired by a Hawaiian dish. ❖ But the pairing of Mom's famous three vinegar shrimp, a Chinese-inspired stir-fry, with mashed potatoes no longer feels outre. Instead, it feels heavy. The shrimp are served in a zingy brown sauce, but after a few bites from the heaping plateful, your taste buds begin to grow weary. Less sauce would let the flavors of the shrimp and vegetables shine, something palates 10 years older and wiser have come to desire. ❖ That sake-miso butterfish is a Blue Ginger classic for a reason. The fish is light and moist and, indeed, buttery, the white flesh sweet from the miso marinade. Blue Ginger is also known for its garlic-pepper lobster, and it's easy to see why. The lobster carapace stands at attention, stuffed with lemongrass fried rice, its meat removed and laid out before it. Bright green pea tendril salad cuts through the butter coating the lobster. ❖ What does feel new at Blue Ginger is the lounge menu. The dishes are smaller, lighter, brighter in flavor. They are more playful than the dishes on the dining room menu: The signature offering here is "Ming's Bings," which are sort of like Chinese Hot Pockets — round, slider-size, dumpling-esque skins stuffed with meat. They come in four flavors: ginger pork and scallion, blue cheeseburger and bacon, roast duck, and mushroom-tofu. It's as if instead of opening a second, more casual restaurant, Tsai simply incorporated it into the original. ❖ There's something to be said for classic. There's also something to be said for change.

# OISHII BOSTON

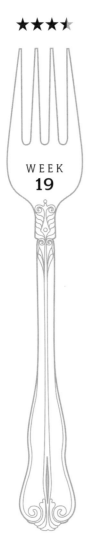

★★★★

**WEEK 19**

1166 Washington St., Boston (South End)
617-482-8868
www.oishiiboston.com
Visa, MasterCard, American Express accepted.
Fully accessible.

**PRICES** Appetizers, soups, salads: $4-$50.
Entrees: donburi $20-$80,
maki and temaki $5-$30. Desserts: $6-$15.

**HOURS** Tue-Sat noon-3 p.m., 5:30 p.m.-
midnight. Sun 1-10 p.m.

**NOISE LEVEL** Several rooms and woven
mats mean sound is kept at a reasonable
level, despite crowds.

## MAY WE SUGGEST

Baby hamachi with fried shallot and
menegi; grilled black pepper-flavored
black pork chop with onion sake sauce;
sudachi and seared hamachi maki; green
tea tiramisu.

TASTING NOTES

IN JULY 2006, sushi master Ting San, who gained fame with a pocket-sized restaurant in Chestnut Hill, brought Oishii to Boston. His South End restaurant is a sleekly-designed space that lacks a sign on the door but is never short of devotees. On any given night, long tables of 20-somethings tuck into maki rolls, while those at the bar chat with Ting as they dangle chopsticks over intricately composed plates of ama-ebi (shrimp) with white asparagus and yuzu, or crispy tuna pancake with arugula salad. Ting's sushi chefs, usually three to five of them behind the counter, bustle about, cutting fish, decorating plates with a curl of daikon, a squiggle of wasabi, a feathery branch of mizuna. ❖ There are many reasons why Oishii works. First of all, there's the greeting. When you walk in, Ting and his chefs stop what they're doing and bow a greeting. Then there's the waitstaff, so enthusiastic that some slow delivery can be overlooked. But most of all, there's the food. It's amazing — and amazingly expensive. Ting has always been known for creativity; here, presentation and finesse are ascendant. ❖ A seared toro sandwich is rich, buttery toro perched on a crisp-edged brown rice chip. Sweet ume (plum) sauce is dolloped on the side, and the play of the toro's fresh, strong flavor against the ume is wonderful. The dish is delicious, and you sigh as you finish the extravagant appetizer. Order hamachi, tuna, ama-ebi, and saku (white tuna) on an ice block and you get a party dish — a block of ice with thin skewers of fish and shrimp protruding from it. ❖ The long menu meanders outside ordinary sushi with entrees such as grilled black pork chop, liberally peppered and fork-tender, and served with an onion sake sauce. A maki roll of Kobe beef and Asian pear contrasts the marbled shavings of meat with the crunch and apple-like flavor of the pear. Scallop maki with a spicy mayo, cucumber, and black tobiko lyrically mingles the delicate flavor of the scallop with the sharp chili notes of the sauce. Some desserts are unusual, too, such as green tea tiramisu, a beautifully-made cake and custard combination sitting in a pool of sweetened green tea. ❖ Despite the delights, there are a few downsides, such as faulty ventilation that allows cooking fumes to waft through the dining room and closely-spaced tables that require the waitstaff to be acrobatic at times. Still, Ting San's regulars and others lucky enough to drop in, Boston Oishii is a treasure.

A.A.

# NO. 9 PARK

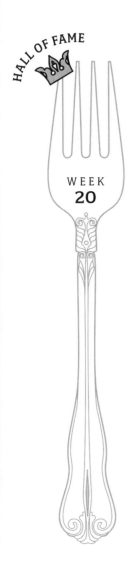

HALL OF FAME

WEEK
**20**

9 Park St., Boston (Beacon Hill)
617-742-9991
www.no9park.com
All major cards accepted. Fully accessible.

**PRICES** Appetizers: $19. Entrees: $39.
Desserts: $12. Three-course prix fixe: $65.
Seven-course tasting menu: $96, $160 with
wine pairings.

**HOURS** Mon-Sat 5:30-10 p.m.; bar area
until 11 p.m.

**NOISE LEVEL** Upholstery and separate
rooms help reduce noise.

## MAY WE SUGGEST

Salad of baby beets with housemade
cow's milk cheese; handmade bigoli with
crab; butter-poached lobster; chocolate
ganache cake.

TASTING NOTES

_____

_____

_____

_____

_____

**BARBARA LYNCH** is a homegrown marvel, a South Boston native who's become a dynamo on the restaurant scene. She started her empire with No. 9 Park and now owns three restaurants, a catering company, a cookbook store, and a produce shop — plus a brand new bar and dining complex in Fort Point Channel. This first one is still a powerhouse on Beacon Hill, the place that garnered her national acclaim and recognition. A visit here is always an event and, even more so, always an adventure. ❖ No. 9 has a slightly subdued, sophisticated look — pale tones, dark wood, a mural of black and white historical photos of the Boston Common matched by a view in the front room of that city oasis of green. The service, too, is pleasingly warm but decorous, and the waitstaff is unusually knowledgeable about food and wine. Cat Silirie's wine selections are so entrancing that it's difficult to let go of the list. As well as selections for connoisseurs, she also offers bottles that are reasonably priced. ❖ You might expect the cuisine to be set in stone in a restaurant that opened in 1998, but Lynch's creativity shines in every season. Appetizers might be baby beets with housemade cow's milk cheese and ras el hanout spicing, or terrine of foie gras with pepper relish. Lynch has said she views each appetizer as a meal in itself, and her compositions show that. ❖ Pasta, always made on the premise and often by Lynch herself, is not to be missed. This includes bigoli, a shape slightly thicker than spaghetti, which on a summer menu was sauced with crab, arugula, and lemon. Gnocchi are stuffed with prunes and come with seared foie gras in a vin santo glaze. She and her staff do justice to tricky seafood entrees such as swordfish with ratatouille jus and olives, and to luxurious meats that include loin of veal with roasted black fig. But then Lynch can throw in an earthy glazed pork belly with turnips and wild purslane to delight the palate. Or wow the splurger with a butter-poached lobster in a lobster and saffron nage. ❖ The splurger wouldn't want to miss dessert, either. Milk chocolate creamsicle with a hazelnut gateau and caramelized banana, a citrus and ricotta custard, a decadent chocolate ganache cake — each one is temptingly worth the calories. ❖ With her strong sense of place in this old building, Lynch has established herself as a Boston phenomenon.

A.A.

# SUSHI-TEQ

★★ ☆ ☆

**WEEK 21**

510 Atlantic Ave., Boston (Financial District)
617-217-5150
*www.intercontinentalboston.com/dining*
*Major credit cards accepted.*
*Wheelchair accessible.*

**PRICES** *Maki: $3-$15.*
*A la carte sushi and sashimi: $8-$15.*
*Omakase sushi: $22 (6 pieces) or $28 (8 pieces).*
*New Age sushi-esque creations: $16-$23.*

**HOURS** *Tue-Fri noon-3 p.m., 5-11 p.m. Sat 3 p.m.-midnight. (Sushi is served till 10:45 p.m.)*

**NOISE LEVEL** *Conversation easy, despite salsa and Spanish-language techno.*

## MAY WE SUGGEST

The 510; the Sushiteq; omakase sushi; Mojarita; Don Julio 1942; tequila flights.

**TASTING NOTES**

_____
_____
_____
_____
_____

**DO SUSHI AND TEQUILA** go together? Decide for yourself at Sushi-Teq in the InterContinental hotel, which offers both, and almost nothing else. ❖ The restaurant — which has a lit-up wall that changes color, space-station tables and stools, and a salsa soundtrack — handles each part of its mission well. At first glance, it treats its sushi with a tequila-esque party sensibility. The menu, in a little red Trapper Keeper, opens with the words "WHY SUSHI? IT'S HOT!" (Hopefully not.) It contains a mini-essay on the evolution of sushi, and short lessons on types of sushi, what "that little green ball of paste" on the side is, and what makes good sushi. "The best Sushi will dissolve in your mouth with nary a nibble, bombarding your taste buds with flavor from all directions," it professes. ❖ Paging past the essays, one finds the likes of Pizza de Sushiteq (salmon, tomato, jalapeno, and other frippery on a tortilla — the bites with jalapeno are good, but it's otherwise bland), tuna mozzarella (elevated from "why bother" status by the Korean chili paste gochujang), and a signature roll called the Big Dig. It includes eel, shrimp, avocado, and asparagus, and its pieces are arrayed in an arch, held in place by the sticky rice. Unlike the real Big Dig, however, it only costs $8. ❖ The best of the New Age combinations is the 510, a maki filled with avocado, cucumber, and asparagus, draped in pieces of gleaming white fish. It's refreshingly light, and a bit spicy from jalapenos. Also a winner is the namesake Sushiteq roll, avocado, cucumber, and scallions rolled in a pretty leaf-green wrapper (it's made of soybeans) and topped with spicy salmon. Keep paging through the menu, though, and ingredients such as cheese, hot peppers, potatoes, and garlic chips give way to an a la carte list offering a very respectable array of seafood, from zuwai (snow crab) to tairagai (penshell) to three kinds of eel and five different toro presentations. The fish I sampled was of high quality, and the sushi chefs put together thoughtfully varied omakase plates. This should come as no surprise — Toru Oga of the acclaimed Oga's in Natick designed the menu. ❖ The tequila is of high quality, too. Sushi-Teq offers tequila flights and tequila-based cocktails galore. There are also about 70 sipping tequilas — the Don Julio 1942 is deep and smooth, with the promised notes of pepper and caramel. Sushi-Teq treats its serious tequilas with a sashimi-esque sensibility: They're served to savor without distraction.

D. F.

# EASTERN STANDARD

★★★☆☆

WEEK
**22**

528 Commonwealth Ave., Boston
(Kenmore Square)
617-532-9100
www.easternstandardboston.com
Major credit cards accepted. Fully accessible.

**PRICES** Appetizers, salads, sandwiches:
$7-$15. Entrees: $18-$32. Desserts: $7.
**HOURS** Lunch: Mon-Sat 11:30 a.m.-2:30 p.m.
Sun brunch: 10:30 a.m.-3 p.m.
Dinner: Sun-Thu 5-11 p.m.,
Fri-Sat 5 p.m.-midnight.
**NOISE LEVEL** Can be noisy when busy.

## MAY WE SUGGEST

Frisee salad with soft-boiled egg; sweetbreads; veal schnitzel; Boston cream pie.

TASTING NOTES

_____
_____
_____
_____
_____

**EASTERN STANDARD** could be the template for this century's restaurant successes. Taking up one end of the long Kenmore Square block occupied by the Hotel Commonwealth, the place is big and beautiful. It's open for breakfast, lunch, and dinner. The bar stretches long and invitingly; the cocktails are large, and the wine list varied. The outdoor partly covered patio is perfect on a great day or even on a so-so one. ❖ Although it looks like a brasserie, its reasonably-priced menu ranges all over the place. With pates and terrines, veal schnitzel, liver and onions, and steak frites, the restaurant fits the French standard. But then there are cheeseburgers and grilled cheese and pasta and almost anything else you could want. ❖ The restaurant has a bold ambience, with beautiful details such as tile floors, a long marble bar backed by mirrors, lots of dark wood and leather, and golden-hued light fixtures hanging like big chrysanthemums down the center. It feels cool in the summer, and cozy, despite its size, in the winter. Owner Garrett Harker and his large waitstaff are solicitous and efficient, and the overall feeling is one of comfort. ❖ This is a concept restaurant rather than a chef-driven one. The strengths are in consistency, not in flights of fancy. That's a fine thing when a veal schnitznel shows off a good job of cooking that results in tender veal inside a very crisp crust. Plenty of capers and pepper, along with the piquancy of artichokes, round out the dish. Or a frisee salad sports crispy sweetbreads scattered in among the greens and a soft-poached egg on top. ❖ Roasted king salmon under mustard crust juxtaposes two strong tastes and makes the combination delicious, and buttermilk mashed potatoes underneath provide a pillowy contrast. Braised lamb shank shows off fork-tender meat, and though it's a little heavy, the flavor compensates. That's also true of a hefty pork chop with a creamy mustard sauce and braised cabbage. ❖ Desserts aren't always a strong point at Eastern Standard, but a chocolate mousse is sweet and dense, and a sort of Frenchified Boston cream pie is a lovely treat. In a phone conversation, Harker has suggested that the aim is not to be an authentic French brasserie, but rather to appeal to and satisfy a wide swath of visitors. In its breadth and comfort level in service and pricing, Eastern Standard proves to be a restaurant for all.

A.A.

# HAMERSLEY'S BISTRO

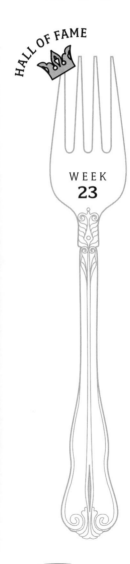

HALL OF FAME

WEEK
**23**

553 Tremont St., Boston (South End)
617-423-2700
*www.hamersleysbistro.com*
*All major cards accepted. Fully accessible.*

**PRICES** *Appetizers: $11-$17.*
*Entrees: $24-$38. Desserts: $9.*
*Brunch: $9-$16.50.*

**HOURS** *Dinner: Mon-Fri 6-10 p.m.,*
*Sat 5:30-10:30 p.m., Sun 5:30-9:30 p.m.*
*Brunch: Sun 11 a.m.-2 p.m.*

**NOISE LEVEL** *Fabric, padding, and enough*
*space make conversation possible.*

## ⊙ MAY WE SUGGEST ⊙

Grilled mushroom and garlic sandwich;
halibut and clam roast with bacon and
braised greens; souffleed lemon custard.

**TASTING NOTES**

_____

_____

_____

_____

**HAMERSLEY'S BISTRO** is a perennial that never loses its luster. That's because of the care and attention that chef Gordon Hamersley and his wife, Fiona, pour into this restaurant. ❖ The Hamersleys were pioneers in the South End, moving into a tiny spot on Tremont in the 1980s when the neighborhood was sketchy and then to its grander location as the area began to be prosperous. Now it's the flagship, and though the late Julia Child, one of the faithful, is no longer around to grace a table in the front, others still fill the place week after week, year after year. ❖ Hamersley's dining room is elegant and restrained, a white tablecloth restaurant that is nonetheless warmly inviting with its pale earth tones. In the summer, the outdoor patio, screened by greenery from the street, makes an inviting oasis along a busy thoroughfare. The waiters, many of whom have worked here for years, are both competent and friendly. And Fiona Hamersley's wine selections are imaginative as well as often good bargains. ❖ The basis of Hamersley's cooking is French, but that is only the starting point. It's a cuisine of myriad influences, reined in by classic style. His flavors have always been assertive but the heaviness that sometimes outdid the boldness in the past seems to have melted away; the result is memorable, attuned to the times and the seasons. Some dishes are classics, such as a delicious grilled mushroom and garlic sandwich on crusty bread, or his famous roast chicken with garlic, lemon, and parsley. ❖ He can transform halibut into a veritable symphony of flavors with clams, bacon, escarole, and black trumpet mushrooms. And he can entrance a vegetarian with a separate menu that includes cold cucumber soup with cherry tomatoes, and wild mushroom risotto with creamy goat cheese and a vegetable ragout. ❖ Sometimes the menu might feature duck roasted with Asian flavorings, or quail bolstered by orange, olives, feta, and fennel. As the restaurant has evolved, more and more American influences have popped up, sometimes in steaks or beef tenderloin, sometimes in grilled tenderloin of pork served with St. Louis style ribs and watermelon. ❖ Desserts slide into the end of the evening with as much grace as the rest of the experience. Crepes filled with blackberry ice cream; warm peach and blueberry cobbler with sweet corn ice cream; or a long-time favorite, souffleed lemon custard, delight any sweet tooth. ❖ In an era of chefs adding multiple restaurants to their resumes, Gordon Hamersley has concentrated his talents on one. And we are the beneficiaries.

A.A.

# HARVEST

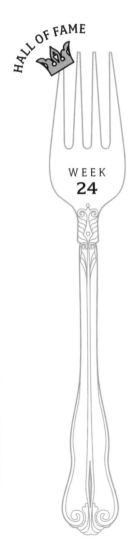

HALL OF FAME

WEEK
24

44 Brattle St., Cambridge (Harvard Square)
617-868-2255
*www.harvestcambridge.com*
*Major credit cards accepted.*
*Wheelchair accessible.*

**PRICES** *Appetizers: $10-$18.
Entrees: $26-$34. Desserts: $8-$15.
Brunch: three courses $35.*

**HOURS** *Brunch: Sun 11:30 a.m.-2:30 p.m.
Lunch: Mon-Sat noon-2:30 p.m.
Dinner: Sun-Thu 5:30-10 p.m.,
Fri-Sat 5:30-11 p.m.*

**NOISE LEVEL** *Conversation easy.*

## MAY WE SUGGEST

Billi bi soup; grilled Long Island duck
breast; crispy braised kurobuta pork
belly "BLT"; Guanaja chocolate souffle
with espresso cream.

TASTING NOTES

**HARVEST HAS TENURE.** The Harvard Square restaurant, feeding and watering hole to the Cambridge intelligentsia since 1975, is assured of its position. But that doesn't mean it's coasting. The food got a major spruce-up in 2008 with new chef Mary Dumont, a onetime best new chef in Food & Wine magazine. ❖ She's the right person to head up Harvest: Her cooking is rooted in the canon, but with a light, modern touch. Not stodgy, not cutting edge, it will impress traditionalists without boring more restless palates. On the current menu, diners find classics such as billi bi soup — little more than mussels, cream, and booze, a throwback both elegant and decadent — duck breast, and rack of lamb. But there's Pernod in the billi bi instead of the usual white wine, lemongrass-prosciutto consomme pooling under the duck, and preserved lemon gnocchi with the lamb. ❖ On Harvest's menu, fruits and vegetables aren't supporting players for protein, they're integral parts of the dish. Grilled duck breast is served in lovely thick, rosy slices, but what makes it so good are the slivers of buttery Verrill Farm pears hiding underneath, a counterpoint in taste and texture. Braised kurobuta pork belly is a quivering cube of fatty, crisp-edged melt-in-your-mouth meat, and if it was served alone on a white plate, it would still command attention. Here it's part of a "BLT" with beans (cannelini), lettuce (braised), and tomato (confit). ❖ Sometimes the elevation of vegetables backfires — salads, for example, can be too lightly dressed. And there's the odd dish that could hold back a bit more; does monkfish really need to be accompanied by herbed stuffing, bacon, artichokes, beans, and cockles, all in a broth heavily dosed with smoked paprika? ❖ But most things work, down to a bourbon pecan tart with a crisp-chewy crust, complemented by dried cranberries, and a chocolate souffle that the server punctures for you, then fills with a little pitcher of espresso cream. ❖ Dumont has composed a menu that reads like a laundry list of local producers and ingredients: In addition to Wolfe's Neck beef and local oysters, you find Applecrest apples, Casco Bay cod, Georges Bank monkfish, and more. It's a bit precious to mention them all, but it also stresses the chef's relationships with regional farmers and fishermen, many of these connections carried over from restaurants at which she previously worked. It gives a sense of continuity. At a place like Harvest, still the quintessential Cambridge restaurant, that seems appropriate.

D.F.

# SHIKI

★★★☆

WEEK
**25**

9 Babcock St., Brookline (Coolidge Corner)
617-738-0200
www.shikibrookline.com
Major credit cards accepted.
Not wheelchair accessible.

**PRICES** Kaiseki lunch: $12-$18.
Small plates: $3-$14. Noodles: $11.50-$14.
Desserts: $3.50-$5.50.

**HOURS** Lunch: Mon-Sat noon-3 p.m.
Dinner: Sun 5-10 p.m.; Mon-Thu 5:30-10 p.m.;
Fri-Sat 5:30-11 p.m.

**NOISE LEVEL** Conversation easy.

## MAY WE SUGGEST

Tsubaki lunch set; chawanmushi; halibut carpaccio; foil yaki; nabeyaki udon; onigiri; ume ochazuke.

TASTING NOTES

_____
_____
_____
_____

SUSHI IS EVERYWHERE, but there's so much more to Japanese cuisine. Shiki is a wonderful place to explore it. And not to worry — it has sushi, too. ❖ Most of the lengthy menu consists of small plates. Several dishes make use of nagaimo and yamaimo, potatoes with an okra-like ooze. They show up in tuna tartare, in soba, and as rounds stacked with pieces of broiled sea eel. Increasing the textural qualities of this eel "mille-feuille" is a poached egg on top — the flavors of the dish are good, but it's difficult to eat without toppling the tower. ❖ Tonkatsu is tender pork cutlets breaded in panko then deep-fried and served on a doily with a nice little mesclun salad. Chawanmushi, a creamy custard served in a pretty black pottery cup, contains hidden surprises: bites of eel, scallops, fish paste, shrimp, and mushrooms. It's a lovely way to start the meal. So is the refreshing halibut carpaccio, thin slices of raw fish treated with olive oil and lemony yuzu juice. ❖ The noodle dish nabeyaki udon is supper for a cold winter night — a big bowl of fat noodles in flavorful broth, with vegetables, fish paste, egg, and shrimp tempura. Foil yaki is a steaming hobo pack of shrimp, Japanese eggplant, kabocha, and more. ❖ But one of the best things at Shiki is also one of the simplest: rice, the building block of Japanese cuisine. It's the centerpiece of the comfort foods onigiri and ochazuke. The former are warm rice balls filled with your choice of spicy orange cod roe, flaky salmon, tart plum, or bonito, then wrapped in toasted seaweed. Of the latter, the plum ochazuke is my favorite: perfect white rice, topped with a leaf of the herb shiso ("perilla" in English), shreds of nori, and plum paste. A blob of wasabi is placed on the side of the bowl for sinus clearing. The waitress brings a teapot of mild broth, and you pour it over the rice. It's soothing, complex, and clean. ❖ For lunch, Shiki offers five different levels of kaiseki, the elaborate, multi-dish traditional cooking. The sets start at $12 and go up to $18; the most expensive one, the tsubaki ("camellia"), includes salad, soup, chawanmushi, tempura, a large platter of sashimi and other small bites, and a bowl of rice. It's an astounding amount of beautiful food for the price. Shiki is a steal, offered artfully. Oh, and the sushi's not bad either.

# DAVIO'S

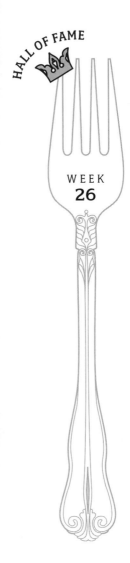

WEEK
**26**

75 Arlington St., Boston (Back Bay)
617-357-4810
*(Now also at Patriot Place, Foxborough,
508-339-4810.)*
*www.davios.com*
*Major credit cards accepted. Fully accessible.*

**PRICES** *Lunch: $6-$25.
Dinner: appetizers $7-$19, pasta $17-$29,
entrees (including steaks) $21-$51,
desserts $8-$12.*

**HOURS** *Lunch: Mon-Fri 11:30 a.m.-3 p.m.
Dinner: Sun-Tue 5-10 p.m., Wed-Sat 5-11 p.m.*

**NOISE LEVEL** *Crowds and high ceilings
make this a noisy place despite padding.*

## MAY WE SUGGEST

Crispy chicken livers with balsamic
glaze; braised short ribs; tagliatelle with
Bolognese; swordfish; panna cotta.

TASTING NOTES

**DAVIO'S** Steve DiFillippo, who was 24 when he opened his first Davio's a couple of blocks away, seems to want to be all things to all people — and many respond. Even on a weeknight, the bar hums with activity, the private dining rooms are filled, and the dining room is bustling. On any given night, the roomy space on Arlington Street will be stocked with sports notables, CEOs, and maybe a music or movie celebrity. ❖ Part of the success can be laid to a battalion of managers and waiters who respond quickly to questions, requests, or complaints. The wine service is helpful and without attitude, and often DiFillippo himself will be the one wishing diners goodnight. The high-ceilinged dining room with its deeply cushioned chairs and large windows is a comfortable place to be, and the colors are soothingly muted taupes and chocolate browns. ❖ Davio's menu is all-encompassing with long lists of antipasti, entrees, and steaks and chops. The cuisine is a sort of relaxed Northern Italian with some steakhouse thrown in, and, luckily, most of it is very good. Take one of Davio's classics: crispy chicken livers in balsamic glaze. The ingredients are humble, but the texture and flavor are exquisite, a crunchy exterior and creamy inside. Bolognese is all the rage these days, so it's a good idea to try it here to have a benchmark for deeply flavored meat sauce of veal, beef, and pork. Other pasta dishes such as jumbo shrimp with hot peppers, garlic, lemon, and fusilli or hand-rolled gnocchi with garlic and roquette offer bright tastes and hearty portions. ❖ Even so, it's the main courses that shine. Short ribs on winter menus are braised so slowly that the meat practically melts on the tongue. Seared salmon has a lively accompaniment of eggplant caponata. Pan-roasted haddock is buttressed by a clam and chorizo sausage stew. ❖ Davio's does well by simple prepared cuts of meat and fish, from a mammoth grilled veal porterhouse to grilled sushi grade tuna. There are plenty of sides, almost none of them plain, including green beans with guanciale (pork cheek), potatoes mashed with gorgonzola, and macaroni and cheese with truffle oil. Desserts, too, are splurges here — from well-made Italian classics such as panna cotta to rich chocolate confections. ❖ This is probably not the place to sample the most cutting-edge cuisine. But the care and aplomb with which the food and the service is handled make Davio's an ideal place for upscale Italian comfort food.

# LEGAL SEA FOODS

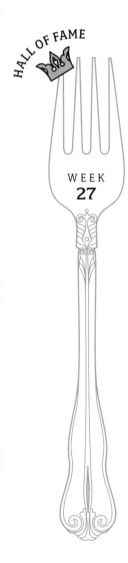

HALL OF FAME

WEEK
**27**

*Numerous locations in Greater Boston and beyond.*
*www.legalseafoods.com*

## LTK ★★★★

*225 Northern Ave., South Boston*
*617-330-7430*
*www.ltkbarandkitchen.com*
*Major credit cards accepted.*
*Wheelchair accessible.*

**PRICES** *Appetizers, salads: $4.95-$12.95. Entrees: $9.95-$28.95. Desserts: $6.*

**HOURS** *Sun-Wed 11 a.m.-1 a.m., Thu-Sat 11 a.m.-2 a.m.*

**NOISE LEVEL** *Can be loud on busy nights.*

### MAY WE SUGGEST

Raw oysters; grilled tuna nicoise; chicken and shrimp omelet wok; big chocolate cake.

TASTING NOTES

 56

**L**EGAL SEA FOODS has been a Boston institution for decades, ever since the original Legal's opened in Cambridge's Inman Square with bare bones decor, long wooden communal tables, and fantastic fish. By now the Berkowitz family has a chain of restaurants that seem to clone themselves all over Boston and down the East Coast to Florida and beyond. The menus — strong on good fish, hearty portions, and surprisingly diverse wine lists — are similar no matter where you are. But a new kid on the Legal block, LTK, a.k.a. Legal's Test Kitchen, is aiming to change the view of the seafood stalwart. ❖ For starters LTK is in the still-raw Seaport area, where mammoth buildings and swooping seagulls outnumber passersby. After a slow start, the sleekly designed place with its technological gadgets seems to have caught on, judging from the crowds around the bar on a weekend evening. ❖ LTK's menu is designed to appeal to a wide swath of diners. There's more emphasis on meat — burgers, Cubano sandwiches of pork, and steak —than at a regular Legal's, as well as dishes such as chicken and shrimp omelet stir fry, pizzettes, and even lamb gyros. It's possible to get a small plate, called nosh, and a glass of wine or beer and get out the door for under $25, making the place especially appealing to younger city dwellers. Still, fish is what draws most people. A grilled tuna nicoise features slices of pink fish over salad greens and oven-dried cherry tomatoes. It's much more appealing than a whole grain fusilli pasta dish with vegetables. ❖ At any of the Legal's, creamy, rich, and full-of-clams chowder may define the ideal of this very classic New England concoction. Oysters, clams, and other raw delicacies are a Legal's speciality. And on any given night you can watch the lobsters — baked, steamed, or stuffed — fly out of the kitchen. Legal's can also refresh a tried-and-true dish such as baked haddock. The fish, simply sprinkled with seasoned crumbs and carefully baked so that no moisture is lost, still tastes of the sea. For years, Legal's has dabbled with Chinese flavorings and Cajun-style spices, but those innovations don't outshine the simpler preparations. ❖ Desserts at both LTK and the Legal's branches lean toward sweet and indulgent — profiteroles, cheesecakes, chocolate cakes — a veritable display of American tastes. The ambience at LTK or any Legal's can be chaotic, and often the waitstaff seems overwhelmed. Presentation and other niceties, too, can be awkward or lacking. Yet where would we be without Legal's?

A.A.

# ANGELA'S CAFE

★★★☆

*131 Lexington St., East Boston*
*617-567-4972*
*Major credit cards accepted.*
*Wheelchair accessible.*

**PRICES** *Appetizers: $2-$8.95.*
*Entrees: $5.95-$12.95. Dessert: $3.95-$5.95.*

**HOURS** *Mon-Sat 7 a.m.-9 p.m.,*
*Sun 7 a.m.-3 p.m.*

**NOISE LEVEL** *Conversation easy.*

WEEK
**28**

## MAY WE SUGGEST

Guacamole; sopa azteca; rajas con
crema; tinga tostada; enchiladas verdes;
mole poblano.

TASTING NOTES

Mex

**THERE ARE MANY THINGS** we do well in New England. Clams fried and chowdered, lobsters rolled and boiled, Fenway franks, roast beef sandwiches. Mexican, not so much. ❖ But there are exceptions. Take Angela's Cafe, a family-run restaurant in East Boston. Chef Angela Atenco Lopez cooked professionally in Puebla, a center of Mexican gastronomy and her home till a few years ago. She now prepares the dishes of that region here (plus the likes of pancakes, steak bomb subs, and ziti). From her tinga to her astounding mole, this is Mexican soul food. ❖ Each night Atenco Lopez cooks what she's in the mood to cook, depending on what's in the larder. There's a printed menu of tacos, quesadillas, and tostadas, all always available. Then there's a chalkboard with a rotating roster of specials. And then there are the other specials, not written down, which her son Luis Garcia tells you about at your table. ❖ Angela's Cafe will have you at guacamole. Just avocados, lime, salt, cilantro, and bit of white onion, it has a silky, chunky texture. ❖ A bit of restraint is in order, though, because there's sopa azteca, a restorative bowl of broth, avocado, and tortilla strips, sprinkled with queso fresco. There's pozole, a soup studded with hominy, pork, and radishes. There are rajas con crema, strips of poblano peppers cooked in cream. And there are endless tasty versions on the theme of something-on-a-tortilla. ❖ Gorditas come in chicken and chorizo versions on handmade tortillas, thick, fresh-tasting pats of masa. A tinga tostada showcases tomato-and-chipotle-tinged shredded beef, lettuce, beans, cheese, and avocado. ❖ Enchiladas are excellent in a green sauce of tomatillos, cilantro, and jalapenos. You can also get them topped with mole poblano, and mole, let's face it, is what you've been working toward all meal: the pinnacle of Angela's kitchen. ❖ There are 50 to 60 ingredients in this sauce. Among them are about 10 varieties of chili, but their heat adds up to a bear hug, not a sucker punch. You can't consciously taste each spice, the tortillas, the plantains, but subconsciously you sense all of the components playing on your tongue. ❖ Angela's Cafe isn't perfect. The mole is also served on chicken breast with rice and beans, but the chicken occasionally comes out dry. One night the pipian tastes off, as if the sesame seeds are on the brink of their expiration date. (Though on another visit it tastes perfectly fresh.) ❖ And if you don't know your way around East Boston, it can be hard to find. But once you home in, you won't forget how to get there. Angela's is memorable.

D.F.

SOMERVILLE · BEYOND

# ROCCA KITCHEN & BAR

★★★★

WEEK
**29**

500 Harrison Ave., Boston (South End)
617-451-5151
www.roccaboston.com
All major cards accepted.
Wheelchair accessible.

**PRICES** Tastes: $4-$9. Appetizers: $7-$13.
Pastas: $10-$17. Entrees: $19-$26.

**HOURS** Dinner: Sun-Thu 5:30-10 p.m.,
Fri-Sat 5:30-11 p.m. Late-night menu:
Mon-Sat 10 p.m.-1 a.m.

**NOISE LEVEL** Jovial.

## MAY WE SUGGEST

Wild mushroom toasts; San Remo
pizzetta; hand-rolled trofie; capellini;
roasted whole fish; Pacciugo di Portofino.

**TASTING NOTES**

**AT ROCCA KITCHEN & BAR,** the cuisine of coastal Liguria is served under a curvy, shade-shifting light strip set into the ceiling. An undulating shape that suggests a river or a map of Liguria itself, the fixture is simultaneously organic and glitzy. The same could be said for this restaurant. ❖ On one hand, Rocca serves straightforward regional dishes for relatively short money. On the other, the restaurant, always buzzing, is filled with people who look like extras from either "Ally McBeal" or "The Sopranos." They're glossy; the food's not. ❖ Take, for example, the trofie. A bowl of pasta with pesto, it looks simple, like something you might whip up with an assist from Barilla. The tadpoles of dough are hand-rolled and assertively al dente, and the fresh, pleasingly coarse pesto is made traditionally, with a mortar and pestle, according to Michela Larson, who co-owns Rocca with Gary Sullivan and Karen Haskell. ❖ The capellini is simple too, adorned with tiny, tender clams still in their purple-lipped shells. The taste is clean: garlic, parsley, and the sea. Any additional ingredient would muck it up. ❖ And when Rocca tries to get fancier, mucking often ensues. Panzotti, triangular dumplings filled with ricotta, struggle in a walnut sauce that begs for a note of brightness. Veal involtini, meat roll-ups stuffed with mozzarella and prosciutto, are dry, the meat lacking flavor. (The accompanying tomato sauce, however, tastes like pureed summer.) ❖ Meat seems to be a stumbling block; vegetables fare better. Wild mushroom toasts; a pizzetta with tomatoes, chopped olives, and anchovies; and gnocchi with seasonal vegetables all do right by produce. ❖ But seafood is Rocca's strongest suit. The bouillabaisse-like buridda is zippy with garlic and features clams and head-on shrimp, with little toasts tucked in, sopping up the broth. And the roasted whole fish competes with the capellini to be the best thing on the menu. ❖ Rocca is uneven, from the salting of the food to the service and design. A horseshoe bar, cork walls, separate levels for drinking/nibbling and dining, and an extremely pleasant patio all work. But the rooms feel overthought and hotel-bland. ❖ The South End restaurant's secret weapon is that it has a parking lot. Good cocktails don't hurt, either. And Rocca is fun; it has energy and, for dessert, a giant sundae with a classy name, Pacciugo di Portofino. ❖ People were excited for this restaurant to open; now they are excited to be here. More than the food, that's what makes it a bright light in Boston's sometimes subdued restaurant scene.

D.F.

# LUMIERE

★★★☆

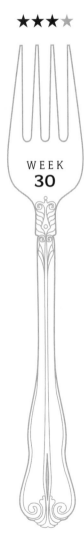

WEEK
**30**

*1293 Washington St., Newton*
*617-244-9199*
*www.lumiererestaurant.com*
*All major cards accepted. Fully accessible.*

**PRICES** *Appetizers: $10-$17.*
*Entrees: $25-$35. Desserts: $8-$10.*

**HOURS** *Mon-Thu 5:30-9 p.m., Fri 5:30-10 p.m.,*
*Sat 5-10 p.m., Sun 5-9 p.m.*

**NOISE LEVEL** *Can be loud in small room,*
*especially in front of kitchen.*

## MAY WE SUGGEST

Peekytoe crab cake with corn, green
tomatoes; cauliflower soup; naturally-
raised beef with garlic creamed spinach;
chocolate fondant cake.

TASTING NOTES

_____

_____

_____

_____

**LUMIERE IS** a most captivating restaurant, engaging all the senses from the moment one pushes the spoon-shaped handles on the front door to the last bite. Here Michael Leviton, the chef and owner, carefully crafted long-held dreams into this little gem, one of the first to show that fine food could be found outside Boston's city limits. No element seems left to chance, and all the little pieces work well together. The food is really lovely; nothing outlandish or outre, but almost all of it good to eat. ❖ There's always something to look at: Beautiful gauze-like fabric covers the windows and doors; the shadow of a fork cleverly decorates the simple menu; Scrabble tiles demarcate the restrooms. The wine list proffers reasonably priced wines that are interesting and work well with the food. The waitstaff is quiet, cheerful, and attentive. ❖ Leviton has said he had a simple bistro in mind when he opened in 1999, but his cuisine is much more evolved than that explanation might indicate. The first spoonful of the cauliflower-leek soup proves the point. The silken concoction tastes clean and vegetal and incredibly rich. A clump of lobster spritzed with rice wine and ginger gives the soup depth, the sweetness of the shellfish made tangy with its seasonings. It's just soup, but it has many layers of flavors. ❖ Leviton's attentiveness really shows up in entrees where he pulls incredible depth of flavor from simple ingredients. His summer menu reads like a farmers' market list — Chatham bluefish and striped bass, zucchini and corn from Verrill Farm, Northeast Family Farm beef. He changes his menu often, but in subtle ways. Carefully roasted chicken might be accompanied by potatoes, mushrooms, and pearl onions in winter, and then by summer be backed by a saute of corn, caramelized onions, bacon, and basil. The steak entrée covers the bases that a steakhouse might, with garlicky creamed spinach and French fries, but adds an interesting balsamic sauce — and at around $30 is much more reasonable than a steakhouse's a la carte offerings. ❖ Lumiere's space was once a Brigham's ice cream parlor, and Leviton offers at least one dessert each season as a tribute, whether it's a root beer float or a raspberry lime rickey float with lime sorbet. A deeply intense chocolate fondant cake fills the need to appeal to the inevitable chocolate fanatics. Lumiere is a place where one wants to be — for Leviton's food, for the warm ambience, for the feeling of a venture well-conceived and well-executed.

A.A.

# GREZZO

★★★☆

WEEK
**31**

69 Prince St., Boston (North End)
857-362-7288
www.grezzorestaurant.com
Major credit cards accepted.
Not wheelchair accessible.

**PRICES** Appetizers: $8-$13.
Entrees: $19-$24. Desserts: $7-$12.
Chef's tasting: $59.

**HOURS** Wed-Sun 5-11 p.m.

**NOISE LEVEL** Conversation easy.

## MAY WE SUGGEST

House salad; gnocchi carbonara; papaya
pappardelle; rich brownie sundae.

TASTING NOTES

_____

_____

_____

_____

_____

**GREZZO IS A** raw food restaurant (and vegan, and mostly organic) — no ingredient here ever gets warmer than 112 degrees, the temperature at which enzymes are said to be destroyed. The raw food diet is heavy on fruits, vegetables, nuts, sprouts, and seaweed — "living" foods — and adherents claim it brings substantial benefits for health and well-being. The restaurant's name is Italian — it means "raw" — and it does serve pasta of a sort: its gnocchi is made from nuts and dressed with "creamy rawmesan," a faux cheese sauce made from more nuts. Still, when Grezzo opened, it seemed a stretch for the North End, an area that draws those in search of piping hot noodle dishes topped with grated realmesan. Nonetheless, on each visit, Grezzo is busy. ❖ The servers are excellent advertisements for their product — they exude serenity, have glowing skin, and smile unflaggingly. But they don't evangelize about the benefits of raw and living food unless you ask. Instead, there's a laminated card titled "40 reasons to eat raw" on each table. ❖ The lack of overt preaching means you can eat at Grezzo for 40 reasons, or for one: the food. ❖ A creamy white corn soup tastes mostly of almond milk, the flavor of the kernels pealing softly in the distance. It's dusted with cayenne and contains refreshing chunks of jicama and avocado. Gnocchi carbonara is good, provided you erase any preconceptions of "gnocchi" and "carbonara" from your mind. The dumplings are made from cashews, pine nuts, garlic, and lemon; they're topped with pea shoots and raw English peas, plus rawmesan — a blender sauce of macadamia nuts, garlic, and oil — for creaminess. ❖ Many of the dishes rely on faux cheese made from nuts. These substances have their moments, but real fruits and vegetables shine. The house salad, for example, is a huge mound of greens with thin rounds of radishes, maroon carrots, and sprouts galore. The almond pulp croutons appear for a soft crunch, and sprouted chickpeas prove addictive. ❖ The papaya pappardelle is also excellent, an extension of the Southeast Asian salads featuring the fruit. Here it's shaved into noodles that are tossed with a creamy tarragon and mustard "thermidor," fresh garbanzos, haricots verts, and currants. ❖ For dessert, there's a brownie sundae. The cake is made from nuts, dates, and raw cacao — fruity and fudgy and dense. It's topped with gelato made in house from nut milk, studded with tiny, slightly bitter, intriguing chips that taste like raw cacao. Mango and strawberry purees complete the picture, along with a magically melted chocolate sauce — how did they do that?

D.F.

# MYERS+CHANG

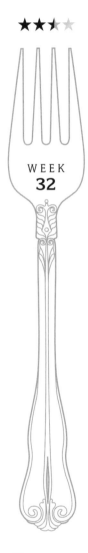

★★★☆

WEEK
32

1145 Washington St., Boston (South End)
617-542-5200
www.myspace.com/myersandchang
Major credit cards accepted.
Wheelchair accessible.

**PRICES** $5-$26. (Daily specials $30-$40.)
**HOURS** Sun-Wed 11:30 a.m.-10 p.m.
Thu-Sat 11:30 a.m.-11 p.m.
**NOISE LEVEL** Rock 'n' roll, baby.

## MAY WE SUGGEST

Esti's hot and sour; tea-smoked pork
spare ribs; braised pork belly buns; tiger's
tears; whole lobster with coconut curry.

TASTING NOTES

**THE BRAINCHILD OF** restaurateurs Christopher Myers (Radius, Great Bay, Via Matta) and Joanne Chang (Flour) is lovable, a dim sum diner serving up chopsocky style with a big wink. The music is loud, the waiters are interactive, and the food — Asian dishes, mostly Chinese, in smallish portions perfect for sharing — is high in flavor and low in price. (Theoretically, at least. The average cost of a dish is about $9, but it takes restraint to keep from ordering more, and they start to add up.) ❖ Chef Alison Hearn, formerly of B&G Oysters and Ten Tables, has graduated to two woks. Dishes come to your table in the order in which they're ready — your dan dan noodles may arrive before your hot and sour soup, with the dumplings coming at the end, just when you've forgotten you ordered them and are feeling too full to eat another bite. To drink, there's sake, wine, and beer — including one called Butternuts Porkslap Pale Ale — plus red and white sake sangrias. (Though the white mostly tastes like juice; it would be a great brunch cocktail.) House-made sodas come in flavors such as aloe-yuzu and lychee-vanilla. For dessert: complimentary mini macaroons. ❖ The poetically named tiger's tears is a salad of grilled steak mixed with Thai basil, slices of fresh chilies, and a taste-bud-rousing dressing of fish sauce and lime. It's addictive. So is Esti's hot and sour, a soup named for Myers's best friend and business partner Esti Parsons. The broth is peppery, gingery, quite sour, and well balanced, just as hot and sour soup should be. It's also the consistency of soup, not pudding. Stick your spoon in and it falls right over — look, Ma, no cornstarch. ❖ It's a kinder treatment of beef and noodles than the beef and broccoli chow fun, which is a disappointment. There's too much beef and not enough noodles, the pieces of stalky Chinese broccoli are sometimes fibrous, and the whole thing is far too greasy. ❖ Dumplings, too, are sometimes greasy; spicy silky tofu isn't particularly silky. But disappointments here are few. Try the sticky, charred, tea-smoked spare ribs; the braised pork-belly buns, slightly sweet and enticingly spongy; and the refreshingly cool Thai ginger chicken salad. ❖ The dishes here aren't formal, they're not always authentic, they're just the kind of thing you want when you're out to enjoy a casual night with friends. Myers+Chang knows how to have fun with chow.

# BENATTI

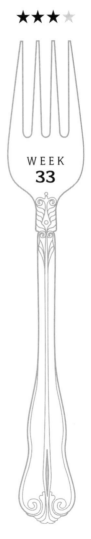

★★★☆

WEEK
**33**

1128 Cambridge St., Cambridge
617-492-6300
*www.benattispecialities.com*
*Major credit cards accepted.*
*Wheelchair accessible.*

**PRICES** *Antipasti: $11-$15. Pasta: $20-$22.
Entrees: $27-$36. Desserts: $12-$14.*

**HOURS** *Mon-Sat 6-10 p.m.*

**NOISE LEVEL** *Conversation easy.*

## ◦ MAY WE SUGGEST ◦

Grilled vegetables; porcini risotto;
tortelloni in balsamic vinegar and walnut
sauce; roasted pork; yellow-tail snapper;
Negroni terrine.

TASTING NOTES

**BENATTI IS LOCATED** on the stretch of Cambridge Street exiting Inman Square, home to many excellent Portuguese and Brazilian restaurants. It's a chic addition, with cool gray paint, modern furnishings, and an elegantly laconic menu: three antipasti, seven pasta dishes (and one exquisite risotto), five well-turned entrees, and six desserts. ❖ The restaurant is named for Italian-born chef-owner Andrea Benatti; he and general manager Anna Encarnacao relocated from Key West, where the couple worked at his restaurant Opera until city life called them away. ❖ Together they've created a charming package. The food is sometimes perfectly simple, sometimes gently innovative, and always genuine; the wine list is all Italian. The space is intimate, with room for about 25 guests among the two-tops and the larger surfboard-shaped table by the window. A tiny butcher-block bar offers a view of the kitchen, where Benatti stands at the stove, flames erupting occasionally from his frying pan. When there's a lull, he'll step out to ask how your meal is. ❖ It's excellent, thank you. An antipasto of grilled vegetables features asparagus, zucchini, red peppers, fennel, and eggplant, striped with grill marks. They are treated with olive oil, salt, and an amazing balsamic from Modena. ❖ Risotto is infused with the deep flavors of demi-glace and porcini. The grains have the exactly right, elusive amount of bite to them. Super-light and fluffy gnocchi dissolve in the mouth, leaving a hint of earthy potato flavor on your tongue. Tortelloni are pillowy dumplings of mild ricotta and spinach, in a balsamic and walnut sauce that is one giant power chord of flavor: sharp, sweet, harmonic. The pasta is handmade each morning for dinner that night. ❖ Slices of roast pork fan out like collapsed dominoes. In a golden rosemary sauce, adorned with a rosemary branch, they face off against a rectangle of lasagna on the plate. The pork is cooked a shade past rosy, and it's delicious. ❖ For dessert, a Negroni terrine looks like pate, tastes like Campari and bitter orange, and is the best dessert I've had in a while. ❖ On many nights, Encarnacao handles the front of the house by herself, playing hostess, waitress, and sommelier while Benatti cooks. It feels as though they've invited you to their place for dinner. ❖ It's an invitation you should accept. This is the kind of food you think about long after it's gone.

# KO PRIME

★★★☆☆

**WEEK 34**

90 Tremont St., Boston (Ladder District)
617-772-0202
www.koprimeboston.com
Major credit cards accepted.
Wheelchair accessible.

**PRICES** Appetizers: $2-$20.
Entrees: $24-$90 (and up). Sides: $6-$9.
Desserts: $10-$13.

**HOURS** Breakfast: Mon-Fri 6:30-10 a.m.
Brunch: Sat-Sun 8 a.m.-12 p.m.
Dinner: Daily 5:30-10 p.m.
Bar menu: Daily 10 p.m.-midnight.

**NOISE LEVEL** Conversation easy.

## MAY WE SUGGEST

Bone marrow; filet mignon with chimichurri; Japanese wagyu beef NY strip; chocolate bread pudding.

TASTING NOTES

**CHEF KEN ORINGER'S** steakhouse does what you'd expect a Ken Oringer steakhouse to do: it serves high-quality meat and sides prepared in ways you won't see at Outback. Filet mignon goes to Argentina with a topping of chimichurri, cutting the richness with tang. Thin slices of skirt steak, amazingly tender, are edged in North African spices. Creamed spinach becomes creamy spinach with mascarpone. The twists here are more conservative than those at his restaurant Clio — they build on steakhouse tradition rather than reinventing it. ❖ Located in the Nine Zero Hotel, the restaurant feels luxe but adheres to the hard-times ethos of not wasting any part of the animal. It serves bone marrow, head cheese as part of a charcuterie platter, and sweetbreads; the décor itself could be classified as Cow Revival. Floors are covered in furry squares of hide, there are Holstein-patterned settees, and the placemats are buttery brown leather. ❖ That bone marrow concentrates the essence of beef; as the runny globs of gelatin dissolve, their richness spreads smoothly across the tongue. It's served in three pieces of bone, alongside stewed oxtail that's just as intensely flavorful and gives you more to chew on; mustard and pickled shallots are acidic counterpoints. ❖ Japanese wagyu beef New York strip makes filet mignon seem tough by comparison — it's velvety and absurdly luxurious. It also costs $30 an ounce, with a 3-ounce minimum. The other entrees are considerably less, but with sides ordered separately and most bottles of wine more than $100, a meal at KO Prime can turn into a real indulgence. ❖ While you're indulging, beef is what to order. Rack of lamb is fine but somewhat boring, and a pork shoulder is coated in an unpleasantly bitter coffee glaze. From the 30-ounce rib eye chop to the Kobe flat iron with romesco sauce, we don't find a dud among the steaks. ❖ The sides are Oringer and executive chef Jamie Bissonnette's chance to be more offbeat, and Okinawa sweet potatoes are just that. The purple mash tastes kind of like bean paste; it would be better in a Japanese dessert than with steak. But the other sides are more standard, mainly variations on a theme of spuds: frites, gratin, baked, but not mashed. Vegetable options include ginormous stalks of asparagus with hollandaise, and pea greens that are far too salty (a recurring issue here) but cooked perfectly and redolent of ginger. ❖ Steakhouse desserts can seem like an afterthought, but here they don't. The chocolate bread pudding is meltingly intense. ❖ With decadent touches here and unusual ingredients there, KO Prime balances opulence and edge.

D.F.

# HIGHLAND KITCHEN

★★½★

WEEK
**35**

150 Highland Ave., Somerville
617-625-1131
*www.highlandkitchen.com*
*Major credit cards accepted. Wheelchair accessible.*

**PRICES** *Appetizers: $3-$9.95. Entrees: $6.95-$19.95. Desserts: $6.*

**HOURS** *Daily 5-11 p.m.*
*Sun brunch 11 a.m.-2:30 p.m.*
*Reservations for parties of six or more Sun-Thu; no reservations Fri-Sat.*

**NOISE LEVEL** *Music loud enough to enjoy, but not so loud that you have to holler.*

### MAY WE SUGGEST

Seafood gumbo; catfish po' boy; goat stew; Highland fish fry.

TASTING NOTES

_____
_____
_____
_____
_____

gastr

**HIGHLAND KITCHEN HAS** one of the best-stocked jukeboxes in town. In fact, music is such an integral part of the Highland Kitchen experience, it may be illustrative to talk about the restaurant and bar in terms of the blues, country, soul, and other eclectic nuggets chef-owner Mark Romano clearly loves. If Highland Kitchen were a playlist, what would be on it?

❖ Let's kick things off with "Soul Kitchen," by the Doors. You can taste the soul in the seafood gumbo, brimming with okra and andouille, deeply flavored from the dark roux at its foundation. You can taste it in the braised pork shoulder with bacon, the tender meat melting into creamy, grits-like polenta.

❖ Plus, the Doors' refrain "I'd really like to stay here all night" seems fitting. With a semi-bare, arty aesthetic — white brick walls, wood floors, chalkboards on the wall, and a long, L-shaped wood bar — Highland Kitchen has an appealing feeling of late-hour cool, even when it's not that late. Neighborhood residents were longing for a real hangout, a place with solid bartending, good food, and a relaxed vibe, and that's what Highland Kitchen delivers. ❖ Next up we have John Lee Hooker doing "Catfish," followed by Junior Wells with "The Goat." The Highland fish fry is a piece of moist, perfectly fried catfish served with hush puppies and remoulade. There's also a craveable po' boy of blackened catfish on baguette, served with sweet house-made pickles. There's a bit of heat to it from cayenne, but it tastes downright mild beside a bowl of curried goat stew on jasmine rice, a version of the dish Romano served in his former post as the chef at Green Street. ❖ Highland Kitchen also has a great cheeseburger and plenty of good bar snacks. What's not to like about a place where you can order deviled eggs and a beer? The eggs are great, with light, relish-studded centers. ❖ The beer list ranges from Miller High Life to Louisiana brew Abita Turbodog to Chimay. The wine list is short, sweet, and reasonably priced. And the mixology is excellent. ❖ Do I hear Tom Waits singing "Chocolate Jesus"? Dessert plays it fairly simple, with chocolate pudding or a moist, just-right slice of chocolate cake. ❖ "It Don't Cost Very Much," by Mahalia Jackson, is music to diners' ears. At $19.95, a grilled salmon special comes closest to breaking out of the teens. ❖ There's only one problem with this gastropub: its popularity. Cue Booker T. & the MG's, singing "You Can't Sit Down."

D . F.

# SCAMPO

★★✦☆☆

**WEEK 36**

1215 Charles St., Boston (Beacon Hill)
617-536-2100
www.scampoboston.com
Major credit cards accepted.
Wheelchair accessible.

**PRICES** *Appetizers: $4-$18. Pizza: $14-$25. Pasta: $12-$22. Entrees: $24-$48.*

**HOURS** *Lunch: daily 11:30 a.m.-2:30 p.m. Dinner Sun-Wed 5:30-10 p.m., Thu-Sat 5:30-11 p.m. Pizza served throughout the day until 1 hour after dinner.*

**NOISE LEVEL** *Conversation easy.*

## ◦ MAY WE SUGGEST ◦

Elephant ear walking; mozzarella with peach and pistachio pesto; burrata and anchovy; baby lamb al forno.

**TASTING NOTES**

_____
_____
_____
_____
_____

LYDIA SHIRE NEEDS a doppelganger. Or a Mini-Me. Or even a hologram. The Locke-Ober chef opened Scampo in the Liberty Hotel just months after opening Blue Sky in York Beach, Maine. How's she supposed to be everywhere at once? ❖ When Shire is in the house, Scampo comes alive. She makes the rounds, a familiar figure with a pouf of mahogany hair and a smile. There's plenty of kissing, and the place looks swell: brick walls, dangling copper-colored bubble lamps, white leather booths in the corner. Behind the shiny orange, U-shaped bar, skilled hands mix excellent Italian mojitos, which are made with prosecco. In the center of it all are pizza and tandoor ovens from which pies and breads issue with regularity. ❖ And when Shire is in the house, the food tastes pretty swell, too. The fancifully named elephant ear walking, a bread almost as thin as a poppadum, arches like a bridge and is topped with tomato and melted cheese. There are seven versions of spaghetti, all available gluten-free, from Bolognese to "e Scampo." This does come with more than one shrimp; in addition to being the singular form of "scampi," the restaurant's name means "escape" in Italian — lest we forget the Liberty Hotel used to be a jail, difficult to do when sitting beneath a giant poster that says "Crime doesn't pay." ❖ A section of the menu is devoted to a fairly firm house-made bufala mozzarella. It's a lovely combination with peaches and pesto made with pistachios. For a creamier take, try the burrata served on little toasts with tomato and anchovies. ❖ The best dish on the menu may be the baby lamb. Roasted whole al forno, it's a Saturday-night special — Friday nights a suckling pig gets the same treatment. On the plate is a piece of meat from each part of the lamb, plus tiny, sweet vegetables. ❖ For dessert, a round of ricotta cheesecake is creamy and light; lemon ice is tart and refreshing. ❖ But when it's not Saturday, when there's no baby lamb, when it's, say, Wednesday and emptier and Shire's nowhere to be seen, Scampo's food can be mediocre. The mozzarella isn't quite as fresh. A plate of the cheese with prosciutto and figs offers exactly 1½ mozzarella slices, a small crime when the dish is filed under "house-made mozzarella." Pizza with mushroom duxelles and homemade ricotta is on the greasy side, and several pasta dishes float in giant pools of butter. ❖ So which restaurant is the real restaurant? Both. You can take your chances; for Scampo at its best, it might be worth it. Or you can wait for Shire to get a Mini-Me.

D.F.

# CODA

★★☆☆

WEEK
**37**

*329 Columbus Ave., Boston (South End)*
*617-536-2632*
*www.codaboston.com*
*Major credit cards accepted.*
*Wheelchair accessible.*

**PRICES** *Appetizers: $6-$10.*
*Entrees: $10-$20.*

**HOURS** *Lunch: Sun 11 a.m.-4 p.m.,*
*Mon-Sat 11:30 a.m.-4 p.m.*
*Dinner: Sun-Wed 4 p.m.-11:30 p.m.,*
*Thu-Sat 4 p.m.-midnight.*

**NOISE LEVEL** *Loud at prime time.*

## MAY WE SUGGEST

Fried calamari; baby arugula, Stilton, and
crispy lardons salad; Black Angus burger;
mac and cheese.

**TASTING NOTES**

_____

_____

_____

_____

_____

**CODA'S NAME IS** a reference to the intersection nearest the bar/restaurant: It's by the corner of Columbus and Dartmouth, in the space once occupied by Tim's Tavern. Its name is not meant to refer to the musical coda, a passage that both prolongs and concludes a movement. Still, this new hangout does extend the legacy of Tim's, which was celebrated most often for its fantastic burger (Coda's is pretty good, too) but also for being a remnant of the "old" South End, before things went and got all fancy. Tim's was the kind of place where everyone felt welcome, and thus everyone went. (Cue "Cheers" theme song here.) But things have changed, too; the space has been spiffed up with paint and a black stone bar top, squishy booths and works by local artists on the walls. So maybe Coda also marks an end: There will be no new dive bars opening in the South End any time soon. ❖ Places like Coda are a fine consolation prize for the loss of sticky floors. The food here is good; the drinks are unstinting; and the service is friendly. And portions are huge. An appetizer or a salad could serve as dinner for someone who's not too hungry, and entrees are likely to also become tomorrow's lunch. ❖ A burger is 10 ounces (or 2½ Quarter Pounders) of black Angus, so proceed with caution. If you should choose to accept this mission, note that asking to have blue cheese slathered on top is not as good an idea as it seems. The stinky cheese overwhelms the flavor of the beef. It will not, however, affect your enjoyment of the excellent, crispy, incredibly salty shoestring fries. ❖ Coda makes arugula salad sinful by adding crispy, salty chunks of pork and Stilton. Ultra-tender fried calamari are tossed with chopped-up banana peppers. ❖ Mac and cheese is not too dry, not too gooey, with the perfect amount of cheese. More of those crispy, salty lardons and some peas are buried among the noodles, breaking up the mushiness. ❖ The only major complaint here is dessert. There are usually two, and they're dull imports from other kitchens, or possibly the freezer aisle. One night the shells on a pair of cannoli are almost too hard to break through, yet also somehow soggy. They're terrible. Otherwise, Coda has a solid formula: strong cocktails, huge portions of food, good burgers, friends and neighbors, all adding up to a low price tag. The new South End and the old South End don't always look that different.

D.F.

# UPSTAIRS ON THE SQUARE

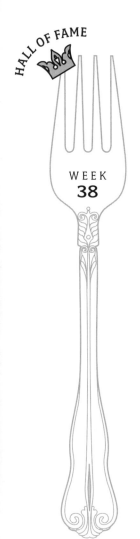

HALL OF FAME

WEEK
**38**

*91 Winthrop St., Cambridge (Harvard Square)*
*617-864-1933*
*www.upstairsonthesquare.com*
*Major credit cards accepted. Fully accessible.*

**PRICES** *Lunch: $8-$18. Brunch: $7-$18.*
*Dinner: Monday Club appetizers $8-$16,*
*entrees $12-$29, desserts $7-$8;*
*Soiree Room appetizers $11-$18,*
*entrees $22-$37, desserts $8-$10.*

**HOURS** *Lunch: Mon-Sat 11 a.m.-3 p.m.*
*Brunch: Sun 10 a.m.-3 p.m.*
*Dinner: Monday Club Sun-Thu 5-10 p.m.,*
*Fri-Sat 5-11 p.m.; Soiree Room*
*Sun-Thu 5:30-10 p.m., Fri-Sat 5:30-11 p.m.*

**NOISE LEVEL** *Monday Club fairly quiet;*
*Soiree Room noisy when crowded.*

## MAY WE SUGGEST

Monday Club: Frisee salad with poached
egg; grilled halibut with Pat's clam and
bacon; ice cream sandwich. Soiree Room:
ravioli of Pierre Robert cheese; seared
Nantucket scallops with creamy fregola;
warm chocolate souffle cake.

TASTING NOTES

**DINING AT** UpStairs on the Square feels as though you've fallen into the midst of a Broadway show, a little like one of those musicals where famous stars burst into song as dancers kick skyward in synchronization. ❖ After losing their 20-year-plus home on Holyoke Street and then searching long for a new location, owners Deborah Hughes and Mary Catherine Deibel caught the brass ring: prime space in Harvard Square. The restaurant, opened late in 2002, displays their exuberance in every aspect — from the wildly decorative design to the ambience and the food. This is a show that stretches over many levels from lunch to dinner to tea to brunch, with wedding catering in between. ❖ UpStairs is really two restaurants: the Monday Club Bar downstairs, with a casual menu; and the much more elaborate Soiree Room several levels up. Hughes designed the place, and her flamboyant persona gleams downstairs in the animal-patterned rugs, green walls hand-striped in pink, and gilded chairs. Then there's the upstairs, where swirls of silver and lilac overlay hot pink walls, and a little service bar in back gleams in Tiffany blue, all of it reflected in mirrored ceilings. ❖ Steven Brand, who cooked for Jean Georges in New York, is the chef, handling a menu that ranges from frisee salad with poached egg in the downstairs club to Nantucket sea scallops with creamy fregola and porcini marmalade upstairs. ❖ Many of the dishes on both floors lean to the rich. Creamy potato gnocchi with duck ragout is a downstairs entrée; upstairs meltingly soft Pierre Robert cheese fills ravioli served with lovage butter, apples, and truffle oil. ❖ A trio of pizzas comes filled with seasonal goodies downstairs. Upstairs, the elaborate décor is matched by luxury items such as sashimi of blue fin tuna with jicama and tempura snap peas, and rib-eye steak with shiso emulsion and truffle vinaigrette. ❖ Desserts match the rest of the production, sweet and elaborate. Downstairs, ice cream sundaes, fruit crisps, and a caramel layer cake satisfy a sweet tooth. Upstairs, there are Meyer lemon baked Alaska and a warm chocolate souffle cake. And on any level, milk chocolate pecan turtles win hearts. ❖ The waitstaff seems to have caught the spirit of the place, generally solicitous and well-informed about the food and wine, and only on rare instances drifting off. The wine list varies from quite affordable to stratospheric. ❖ The old UpStairs was always an effusive place, its fans fiercely loyal, its traditions strong. The new UpStairs, more a re-creation than a revival, is a little dizzying, but often dazzling.

A.A.

# SEL DE LA TERRE

WEEK
**39**

*255 State St., Boston (Long Wharf)*
*617-720-1300*
*\*Additional locations: 774 Boylston St.,*
*Boston (Back Bay), 617-266-8800;*
*1245 Worcester St., Natick, 508-650-1800*
*www.seldelaterre.com*
*Major credit cards accepted. Fully accessible.*

**PRICES** *Lunch: first courses $10-$14,*
*entrees $9.50-$18, three-course prix fixe $21.*
*Dinner: first courses $10-$15,*
*entrees $25-$34, desserts $9.50-$12,*
*three-course prix fixe $45.*

**HOURS** *Daily 11 a.m.-10 p.m. Late-night menu*
*(Boston location): Wed-Sat 10 p.m.-12:30 a.m.*
*Brunch: Sat-Sun 11 a.m.-4 p.m.*

**NOISE LEVEL** *Upholstery and sound-proofing*
*keep down noise.*

## MAY WE SUGGEST

Bread with tomato confit; assiette de
charcuterie with toasted brioche; rabbit
wrapped in prosciutto with mustardy
potatoes; milk chocolate-lavender ice
cream profiteroles.

TASTING NOTES

_____

_____

_____

**SEL DE LA TERRE** opened at the start of the century in the middle of the tangle of Big Dig construction. It seemed a risky — or brilliant — location then. Now, with construction barricades giving way to greenery, this smart but casual restaurant is in an enviable spot with a reputation to match. Owned by Frank McClelland of L'Espalier and Geoff Gardner, the chef, the restaurant with its own boulangerie (bakery) hums from breakfast to late night. ❖ Bread might be a giveaway some places, but here it's almost impossible not to be won over by the goodness of the many varieties offered. Gardner's menu is full of approachable dishes and clear flavors. Compared to McClelland's grander restaurant, where Gardner had long been sous chef, Sel de la Terre is consciously a more everyday kind of place, and its food is straightforward, loosely following a country French theme. ❖ The design of the room — cleverly variegated with dividers, alcoves, and wood and stone flooring — transforms what must have been a blank rectangle into a handsome restaurant. The wine list is broad and has a range of prices with some interesting, affordable French wines. ❖ The restaurant has an unusual pricing system with all the appetizers at one price and the entrees at another; there are also prix fixe options for lunch and dinner. Gardner shows his considerable talent in dishes with clear agendas. A caramelized onion, spinach, and sundried tomato tart hits high notes of Provencal cooking, the onions made appealingly sweet by slow cooking, the sundried tomatoes adding intensity, the spinach and Comte cheese richness. And the crust is just crisp enough and yet tender. He's careful with fish, so that the result is moist and the plate well balanced with seasonal vegetables. Stronger flavors such as rabbit wrapped in prosciutto with a mustardy glaze are well-treated here, as are classic pates and terrines. ❖ Sel de la Terre's pomme frites with rosemary have reached cult status — for good reason, since they're crisp, greaseless, and almost impossible to stop eating. Desserts follow the modernized French model: milk chocolate-lavender ice cream profiteroles with chocolate sauce, creme brulee, a peach upside down cake. ❖ It took a little while for this restaurant to shape up, but just like its neighborhood, Sel de la Terre has become an appealing place to be.

# 51 LINCOLN

★★⯨☆

**WEEK 40**

*51 Lincoln St., Newton*
*617-965-3100*
*www.51lincolnnewton.com*
*Major credit cards accepted.*
*Wheelchair accessible.*

**PRICES** *Food/liquor pairings: $6-$9.*
*Appetizers and pasta: $9-$23.*
*Entrees: $20-$29. Desserts: $6.*

**HOURS** *Sun-Thu 5-10 p.m.; Fri-Sat 5-11 p.m.*

**NOISE LEVEL** *Center of the room can get very noisy.*

## MAY WE SUGGEST

Pan-seared watermelon steak with confit tomatoes; rigatoni bolognese; day-cured salmon with preserved lemon; ice cream, any flavor.

TASTING NOTES

_____

_____

_____

_____

_____

**JEFFREY FOURNIER** waited a long time for his own restaurant. And now, he's spreading his wings at 51 Lincoln, a compact spot where his own artwork is on the walls and the dishes reflect his flirtation with Latin flavors and with highly seasoned small appetizers. The sureness of his technique, with the echoes of the kinds of classics that he has honed over the years, can be dazzling. The wine list sports an interesting array of bottles at quite reasonable prices, with many under $35. ❖ The little Newton Highlands restaurant can feel cramped, the noise explosive, and the waitstaff harried. But concentrating on the food brings rewards. His pan-seared watermelon steak with confit tomatoes is a revelation, giving a whole new character to the fruit. He keeps up the Latin flavors one evening in a special of tuna tartar that sings with lime juice and cilantro. He creates a version of a Caesar salad, thoughtfully arranged so that the lettuce stays crisp, the dressing is tangy, and the made-to-order croutons crunch satisfyingly but are soft in the middle. ❖ Fournier has said he's especially interested in pastas and risottos, which he believes are often not made well despite being on every menu. Take a mouthful of his bolognese with rigatoni, a classic played out on many menus but masterfully done here. ❖ Despite the chef's fondness for small plates such as those he did at the now-extinct Sophia's, 51 Lincoln has a long list of entrees. A plate of salmon looks almost severe: the fish, some asparagus (or, in another season, summer squash), jasmine rice, and a little pool of preserved lemon jam. But then the quick curing in spices, salt, and sugar registers, deepening the flavors of the slightly rare fish. There's nothing unusual about roasted chicken in a thin pan gravy, but the skin is nicely crisp and the flesh moist. The braised short ribs are worth the calories you can feel trickling down your throat with every meaty bite. ❖ At the entrance to the restaurant, a blackboard gives a foretaste of desserts — the ice cream and sorbet specialties made that day. It's good advertising and a sign that this is a course to be taken seriously. A very dense chocolate torte studded with caramelized nuts reinforces that. But the ice creams star — creamy vanilla, a sweet and nutty butter pecan, and slightly tart black raspberry. If 51 Lincoln decided to change gears, there could be a second life as an ice cream parlor.

# GRILL 23 & BAR

★★⯪☆

*161 Berkeley St., Boston (Back Bay)*
*617-542-2255*
*www.grill23.com*
*Major credit cards accepted. Fully accessible.*

**PRICES** *Appetizers: $10-$19.*
*Entrees: $34-$36 (steaks and chops: up to*
*$56). Desserts: $9-$11.*

**HOURS** *Mon-Thu 5:30-10:30 p.m., Fri 5:30-11*
*p.m., Sat 5-11 p.m., Sun 5:30-10 p.m.*

**NOISE LEVEL** *Very noisy on bottom level;*
*upstairs quieter.*

WEEK
**41**

## MAY WE SUGGEST

Prime steak tartare; Atlantic halibut
with shaved mushrooms; Kobe cap steak;
vanilla bean creme brulee.

TASTING NOTES

steak

**GRILL 23 & BAR** is a wildly popular restaurant in a city that seems to have gone nuts for steakhouses. Although competition from locals plus national chains has grown in the last several years, the devotion of its fans keeps the Grill high in the city's beef favorites. ❖ The restaurant's dark wood, Oriental carpets, and heavy hanging lamps bespeak a men's club look, writ large. All the details — from a 900-bottle wine list to thick white linens and heavy silverware — drive home that impression. Service can be a little impersonal at times, especially in the tumultuous bottom floor, but is efficient. Without a doubt, this is place to impress friends and clients. ❖ Although it follows the steakhouse classic order of cuts of meat and fish served plain with side dishes extra, the menu has evolved over the years beyond steaks and chops. Chef Jay Murray offers imaginative seafood and meat dishes and concentrates on sourcing natural and fresh ingredients. Still the best of the appetizers is a classic: steak tartare, blood red, finely minced, and pure carnivore indulgence. Richness isn't just reserved for the luxury dishes; each leaf of Romaine in a Caesar salad drips with an eggy dressing, taking it out of the dieter category ❖ Murray plays with seasonal ingredients, such as soft shell crabs, crisp on the outside and tender within. Striped bass is accompanied by corn risotto and tomatillo sauce. Meat still holds sway: A 16-ounce dry-aged rib eye comes with a twice-baked potato and spinach creamed with cheese and bacon. Slow-roasting proves a good method for tenderloin, which can be too dry if grilled. The drift of mashed potatoes underneath is as finely textured as baby food but tastes purely of potato. If size matters, there are 32-ounce portions of prime rib or 24-ounce porterhouses. But everything pales next to the Kobe rib-eye cap, with its expensive explosion of taste in each bite. ❖ Splurging on the meat doesn't mean final courses are any less extravagant. Desserts are luxury versions of comfort food — a hot fudge sundae with sweet and salty almonds, a decadent cheesecake with local berries, a berry shortcake in summer, or a seasonless vanilla bean creme brulee. ❖ Grill 23's popularity is not just the reputation of the steaks. It's a combination of elements, beef key among them, that include the fact that people gravitate to places where others love to go. The place is too loud, and you can feel like one of the herd at times. But it feels like a party — and the Kobe wins the door prize.

# PERSEPHONE

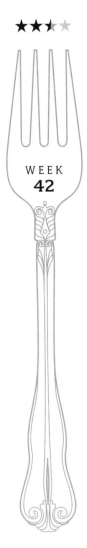

★★⯪☆

**WEEK 42**

*283 Summer St., Boston (Fort Point Channel)*
*617-695-2257*
*www.achilles-project.com*
*Major credit cards accepted.*
*Wheelchair accessible.*

**PRICES** *Small: $1.50-$9.*
*Medium: $12-$30. Large: $26-$29.*
*Extra large: $58-$100. Desserts: $8-$16.*

**HOURS** *Lunch: Mon-Fri 11:30 a.m.-2:30 p.m.*
*Dinner: Mon-Thu 5:30-10 p.m.,*
*Fri-Sat 5:30-11 p.m.*

**NOISE LEVEL** *Cacophonous when busy.*

## MAY WE SUGGEST

Bacon and sea salt pretzel; red curry
chicken wings; duck egg en cocotte;
grilled local squid; grilled chicken.

TASTING NOTES

86

**THE FIRST THING** you see when you enter Persephone are glass cases filled with hanging clothing. The restaurant shares its footprint with the boutique Achilles. ❖ But do fine fabrics and sauteed garlic belong in the same space? You don't want your fashion to smell like food. And you don't want your food to smell like fashion: Restaurant/store hybrids sometimes become more about being there than eating there. ❖ The way to avoid that, it seems, is to enlist someone like Michael Leviton of Lumiere to helm the kitchen. His elegant West Newton bistro is all white walls and white tablecloths. The warehouse-chic Persephone goes in the opposite aesthetic direction — a big, loud space full of exposed brick and bare, dangling light fixtures. Lumiere is a serious restaurant. Persephone is a fun one. ❖ But Leviton is still a serious chef, even when his food takes a playful turn. This adds up to dishes like red curry chicken wings and baked-to-order bacon and sea salt pretzels. The skin on those wings is crisp as phyllo, and the curry that tints them orange is heady with lemongrass and a little heat. The pretzel is a warm knot of dough studded with salt and bits of crunchy meat. It comes with a pot of wonderful house-made apple mustard. ❖ Persephone's menu forgoes the usual categories of appetizer and entree, divided instead into small, medium, large, and extra large. Meat is humanely raised, and ingredients are as local as the season permits. The restaurant recycles, composts, converts used oil into biodiesel, and so on. ❖ The wine still comes from far away — the list is food-friendly and moderately priced. Persephone also has a fantastic cocktail called the Gin & Jazz, a lovely mixture of Hendrick's, vermouth, jasmine tea, cucumber, and lime. ❖ The grilled local squid is a genius of a dish, fresh and bright, the squid with a nice bite, served with chickpeas, preserved lemon, and a parsley salad. Duck egg en cocotte with mushrooms is a runny delight to be mopped up to the last drop with grilled bread. ❖ Things get just a little less interesting when the plates get bigger. Chatham cod with mushrooms is too salty and one-note, despite the ginger and scallions. ❖ Grilled chicken, however, is served with palate-pleasing, balanced components: arugula, pine nuts, golden raisins, and capers. It's a great flavor combination. At Persephone, food comes before fashion.

D.F.

# TOP OF THE HUB

HALL OF FAME

WEEK
**43**

800 Boylston St., Prudential Building,
Boston (Back Bay)
617-536-1775
www.topofthehub.net
Major credit cards accepted.
Wheelchair accessible.

**PRICES** Appetizers: $9-$125 (caviar).
Entrees: $24-$45. Desserts: $9-$13.

**HOURS** Dining room: Lunch Mon-Sat 11:30
a.m.-2:30 p.m.; brunch Sun 11 a.m.-2 p.m.;
dinner Sun-Wed 5:30-10 p.m.,
Thu-Fri 5:30-11 p.m., Sat 5-11 p.m.
Bar and lounge: Mon-Wed 11:30-1 a.m.,
Thu-Sat 11:30-2 a.m., Sun 11-1 a.m.
(brunch and drinks only until 2 p.m.).

**NOISE LEVEL** Conversation easy.

## MAY WE SUGGEST

Clam chowder; pan-seared scallops;
monkfish osso buco; roasted chicken;
freshly baked cookies.

TASTING NOTES

**LET IT JUST** be said. You eat at Top of the Hub for the view — 52 stories above the city — more than the food. But you do hope the food will be good while you're here. It doesn't have to be. The restaurant is always full. Top of the Hub is a special occasion restaurant — a stalwart of New Year's Eves, birthdays, and anniversaries. People will come even if the food is mediocre. ❖ And so the food is exactly as good as it needs to be to keep guests happy. Some dishes are quite tasty. Some are less so. ❖ For example, lobster served in a tempura batter with bok choy, sushi rice, and a gloppy sauce that tastes a lot like La Choy sweet and sour. If the lobster meat tasted fresh, that sauce might be forgivable. But it tastes like nothing. Worse, it smells strongly like ammonia — a bad sign. ❖ But the monkfish osso buco is succulent and satisfying, served with capers, roasted peppers, and olives. The Mediterranean flavors are bold, but the fish is meaty enough to support them. ❖ Roasted chicken is another winner, juicy inside and crisp-skinned. Pork chops, slightly overcooked, get a Southwestern flair with a side of creamy masa and zippy tomatillo cream. The menu isn't particularly adventurous, but it's more so than you might expect. For every bowl of pleasing clam chowder (not too thick, with plenty of potatoes, clams, and pepper), there's a spicy lobster soup with coconut, lemongrass, and ginger. Even the pickiest crowd is pleased, and the chef isn't stabbing himself with his santoku out of sheer boredom. The wine list has a similar aesthetic — two glassed-in wine rooms contain treasures, even as the by-the-glass list trots out chardonnay after chardonnay. ❖ Dessert, too, makes the effort with the likes of caramelized pineapple vanilla bean tea cake with chai ice cream, but the cake is too dry. A plate of cookies baked fresh when you order them is the clear choice. Peanut butter, chocolate chip, and vanilla cookies arrive warm, in large quantities. One night they could have baked longer but are satisfyingly soft. Another, they've been scorched, then dusted with so much powdered sugar we can barely see they're burned. Maybe we just won't notice! We notice. ❖ Top of the Hub recently underwent a renovation, and the place looks swank, painted in chocolate-and-caramel horizontal stripes. It remains a great place to come for a drink. The space, the staff, and the view make dining here feel special. The food doesn't reach the same heights.

D.F.

89

SOMERVILLE • BEYOND

# EAST COAST GRILL & RAW BAR

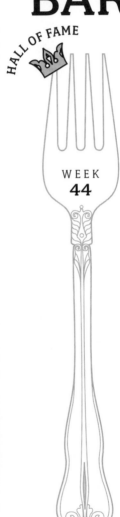

HALL OF FAME

WEEK
**44**

*1271 Cambridge St., Cambridge (Inman Square)*
*617-491-6568*
*www.eastcoastgrill.net*
*Major credit cards accepted. Fully accessible.*

**PRICES** *Appetizers: $5.50-$13.50;*
*raw bar, half-dozen oysters, $13-$14.*
*Entrees: $14.50-$27.50. Desserts: $6.*
*Brunch: $3-$15.75.*

**HOURS** *Dinner: Sun-Thu 5:30-10 p.m.,*
*Fri-Sat 5:30-10:30 p.m. Brunch:*
*Sun 11 a.m.-2:30 p.m. Reservations accepted*
*for parties of five or more.*

**NOISE LEVEL** *This crowded place can*
*be noisy.*

## MAY WE SUGGEST

Oysters on the half shell; buttermilk fried
oysters; grilled spiced mahi mahi;
Eastern North Carolina shredded pork
platter.

TASTING NOTES

_____

_____

_____

_____

_____

90

**EAST COAST GRILL & RAW BAR** opened in 1985 and took the city by storm — the grilling, the hearty barbecue, the easy casualness of the cramped room, the friendly "we're all in this together" feeling. It was a new way of dining then, and if by now that style seems ubiquitous, it's because of Chris Schlesinger and his vision of fun. ❖ Although barbecue was the focus in the early years, the emphasis later shifted to seafood; "raw bar" was added to the name more than a decade ago. The uncomfortably cramped space was enlarged slightly — now it's just crowded. Brightly colored with funky light fixtures and wall hangings, a low-key friendly staff, and a wide variety of menu offerings, East Coast still feels like fun. ❖ Spice is the watchword of the cuisine, and the influences come from everywhere. Ginger and soy flavor tuna; a summer gazpacho has a Caribbean lilt; Old Bay seasons barbequed shrimp served with corn on the cob. A blackboard advertises fish and shellfish that's especially local, from New Bedford scallops to bluefish to Wellfleet clams. Strong flavors are ascendant, even when East Coast isn't holding one of its famed "Hell Nights" focused on chili-laden dishes. Chipotle peppers kick up crispy chicken livers. White-pepper-crusted tuna is served with aged soy sauce and fresh wasabi. Chicken wings are dubbed "wings of mass destruction" and get a coating of Inner Beauty hot sauce, a Schlesinger side venture. ❖ All this heat can make the barbecue seem tame by comparison. But some patrons return time after time just for Memphis-style dry-rubbed pork spare ribs and burnt ends of brisket. And if all this spiciness gets redundant, you can always just come for the oysters and other raw shellfish, abundant and sparklingly fresh. Or have a giant, 16-ounce wood-grilled sirloin with French fries. ❖ This is not the place for subtlety, though, and now and then more delicately conceived dishes seem overwrought — salads with too much dressing, side greens made too limp, bacon added everywhere. Generous portions and hearty flavors win out over pretty plates. ❖ One almost never has room for dessert, and those offered are homey rather than memorable. Maybe it's best to take a walk around the block and then stand in line for ice cream at Christina's down the street. After all, that will give you time to contemplate coming back for East Coast's Latin brunch on Sundays. Tortilla rellenos with smoked duck and queso fresco, or cornbread-crusted French toast with tropical fruit and marmalade, anyone?

A.A.

# AUJOURD'HUI

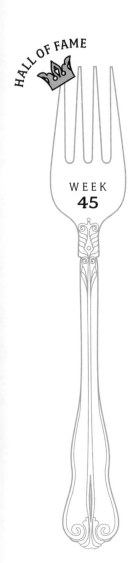

HALL OF FAME

WEEK
**45**

200 Boylston St., Four Seasons Hotel,
Boston (Park Square)
617-351-2071
www.fourseasons.com/boston/dining/
aujourd_hui.html
Major credit cards accepted. Fully accessible.

**PRICES** *Appetizers, salads, soups: $16-$38.
Entrees: $36-$48. Desserts: $12-$20.*

**HOURS** *Dinner: Sun 6-10 p.m.,
Tue-Sat 5:30-10 p.m. Brunch: Sun 11 a.m.-2 p.m.
Closed Mondays.*

**NOISE LEVEL** *Padding and space mean
the room is quiet.*

## MAY WE SUGGEST

Veal sweetbreads with apple vinegar
sauce; pumpkin soup; butter-poached
Maine lobster, parsnip puree; apple tarte
tatin bread pudding with creme fraiche
ice cream.

TASTING NOTES

**AUJOURD'HUI IS AMONG** the stalwarts of luxury dining in Boston. Like one of those million-dollar homes that gets a redo every couple of years, this fine-dining restaurant in the Four Seasons Hotel was refurbished several years ago. Of course, in restaurant life that includes more than just a few new chairs or a paint touchup. The changes helped redefine the place, making the dining room feel more spacious. ❖ And now Aujourd'hui has its own handsome bar at the front entrance, replacing an awkward waiting area. The bar is appointed in dark mahogany and upholstered club chairs, the walls are adorned with old portraits that look like they came out of a Salem mansion. Service has always been a key element here. Black-suited waiters and waitresses hover around each table, their attention finely tuned. Water glasses are never less than full, and the courses are brought seamlessly to the table. The wine list is diverse, long, and expensive. ❖ Aujourd'hui, which no longer serves lunch, has had a succession of chefs over the years, not unusual in a large hotel chain. It has also had a variety of culinary emphases, from hints of Southwestern to Asian fusion to French. William Kovel is executive chef and his menu slants more toward New American than the previous French. He offers veal sweetbreads with Cortland apple puree and an apple vinegar sauce, and pumpkin soup with mostarda fruits for appetizers. Some dishes are de rigueur, such as a butter-poached Maine lobster with parsnip puree. Others are more daring, such as a duo of lamb that includes olive-oil poached tenderloin and confit of tongue. His repertoire hits all the high notes one would expect, such as foie gras terrine with a fig compote, and sea scallops with truffled potato puree and lobster sauce, and it doesn't neglect the vegetarians, offering them a tomato tasting and a cauliflower risotto. ❖ Desserts are as finely wrought as the rest of the dishes. A bittersweet chocolate truffle bar with caramelized banana and latte mascarpone mousse is a showstopper, and for the brulee lover, there's a lemon creme version with roasted strawberries and coconut sorbet. An apple tarte tatin bread pudding gets a topping of creme fraiche ice cream and a sprinkling of fennel-spiced red grapes. ❖ Competition in fine dining has grown more fierce and public taste has become more casual, but this calm and well-managed spot with its view of the Public Gardens can still delight the diner.

A.A.

# VIA MATTA

★★★☆

**WEEK 46**

79 Park Plaza, Boston (Theater District)
617-422-0008
*www.viamattarestaurant.com*
*Major cards except Discover accepted.*
*Fully accessible.*

**PRICES** *Lunch: appetizers $9-$16, entrees $14-$22. Dinner: appetizers $9-$18, entrees $17-$38, desserts $9-$10.*

**HOURS** *Lunch: Mon-Fri 11:30 a.m.-2:30 p.m. Dinner: Mon-Thu 5:30-10 p.m., Fri 5:30—11 p.m., Sat 5-11 p.m.*

**NOISE LEVEL** *Hard surfaces and crowds mean noise.*

## MAY WE SUGGEST

Crudo of yellowfin tuna with crispy zenzaro, avocado and cucumber; swordfish with spicy eggplant caponata; vanilla panna cotta with fruit.

TASTING NOTES

_____
_____
_____
_____

*Ita*

**WHEN VIA MATTA** opened in 2002, the stylish and urbane restaurant was heralded like a rock star and quickly gained local and national fame. It was a heady entrance for any restaurant, even the sibling of Radius, the first trendy spot of owners Michael Schlow (chef) and Christopher Myers. ❖ By now Via Matta (the name means "crazy street" in Italian) has had time to mature. It still can be a scene, the dining room full of well-dressed parties, everyone craning to see who else is in the room; the bar and the wine cafe pulsing with a young set intent on merriment; the wait staff sometimes a little distracted by the crush. Yet this evocation of a big-city restaurant in Italy — with its long, ciabatta-laden wooden tables, distressed wood floors, and etched glass separating the bar and dining room — gets a solid underpinning from the food. The style is modern Italian, clean and spare, with flavor coming from the quality of the ingredients and not too much fuss over sauces or presentation. ❖ That is not to say that Via Matta's food feels peasant-style. A selection of crudo, or raw, and marinated seafood shows off beautiful specimens of yellowfin tuna, lobster, and other luxe ingredients and the prices are scaled to match. Handmade ravioli and other pastas shine in technique and taste. The menu boasts fine examples of cured meats such as sopressata and mortadella. The ricotta is homemade and spiked with sage and hot peppers. ❖ One of the heartening aspects of Via Matta is the prices, not bargain basement by any means, but with enough range so that you can have a simple pasta for under $20 or splurge with sirloin of beef for nearly $40. Side dishes of vegetables are offered a la carte, a trend that has swept from steakhouses to almost all of the new high-level restaurants. However, the plates of delicious roasted cauliflower or broccoli rabe with hot pepper are big enough for a table of four to share. Italian regions dominate the wine list, and though the prices climb steeply, there are also interesting selections under $40. ❖ Italians don't eat dessert like we do — they're more likely to finish with fruit than cheesecake, saving pastry for afternoon coffee break. Via Matta straddles the line. It offers lean treats such as granitas and a few more lavish constructions in fruit and chocolate. The spareness of the dessert offerings reflects the restaurant, its cool glitter backed by the kind of food you'd eat in Italy today.

A.A.

# TROQUET

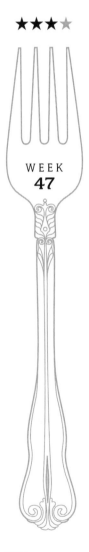

★★★☆

WEEK
47

*140 Boylston St., Boston (Theater District)*
*617-695-9463*
*www.troquetboston.com*
*Major credit cards accepted. Fully accessible.*

**PRICES** *Appetizers: $10-$19.*
*Entrees: $23-$38. Desserts: $8-$10.*

**HOURS** *Tue-Sat 5 p.m.-11 p.m.*

**NOISE LEVEL** *Conversation possible.*

## MAY WE SUGGEST

Duo of foie gras with cherries; slow
poached king salmon with Puy lentils;
chocolate fondant cake.

TASTING NOTES

**ONE OF THE REASONS** we eat out is to experience the sensuousness of matching the taste and textures of food to wine — meltingly rich meat to a rounded red, silky sea-tasting fish to a crisp white. Although most restaurants offer wine with food and many do it expertly, few make that marriage of flavors their principal mission. That's a niche that Troquet is designed to capture. ❖ Co-owner Chris Campbell is well-known for his wine knowledge, and his partner Scott Hebert, who previously cooked at the wine restaurant Veritas in New York, is hailed for his ability to match food to wine. Troquet produces a happy union. ❖ Troquet (the word is French slang for a small wine cafe) has a formal upstairs dining room and a more casual bar downstairs, as well as a brand new desserterie called La Patissier. It's not a lavishly appointed place, but has a reassuring seriousness about it. ❖ The menu is a challenge, not because of the food, which is simply explained, but because of the matching of 40-some wines (served in 2-ounce or 4-ounce glasses). There's also an ever-changing list of wines by the bottle. The pairings are a good idea but not always easy to comprehend in the whirl of conversation at the beginning of a meal when you're catching up with friends and deciding what you might like to order. ❖ Hebert has said that the wines determine the ingredients he chooses. His influences are French and the dishes tend to be rich, such as salmon poached very slowly in olive oil and goose fat, probably knocking out any thought of the dish for a dieter but definitely upping the flavor quotient. Foie gras, poached lobster, roasted suckling pig, and plenty of exotic mushrooms dot the menu, and pan-roasted rib steak can give steakhouses a run for their money. The cheese tray offers nightly treats such as a Vacherin — so creamy as to be almost liquid. And desserts keep up the luxurious feeling with rich chocolate molten cakes and creme brulee. ❖ Troquet's emphasis on wine means this is an unusual place, putting some limits on the cuisine — and its self-description as a wine boutique is apt. It might not be a restaurant where you'd hang out several nights a week, but it's a wonderful option to have in a city where restaurants can all too often blur into sameness.

A.A.

# BIN 26 ENOTECA

*26 Charles St., Boston (Beacon Hill)*
*617-723-5939*
*www.bin26.com*
*American Express, Visa, MasterCard accepted.*
*Fully accessible.*

**PRICES** *Appetizers, soups: $9-$16.*
*Pasta, entrees: $14-$30. Desserts: $9.*

**HOURS** *Mon-Thu noon-10 p.m., Fri-Sat noon-11 p.m., Sun 5:30-10 p.m.*

**NOISE LEVEL** *Small space, hard surfaces, crowds — it all adds up to noisy.*

WEEK
**48**

### MAY WE SUGGEST

Mozzarella wrapped and roasted in speck; cocoa tagliatelle with porcini ragout; rabbit filled with eggplant, funghetto-style; threeramisu (tiramisu three ways).

TASTING NOTES

_____
_____
_____
_____
_____

**BOSTON REALLY NEEDED** a chic Italian wine bar. That seems obvious when you see the throngs pushing into the sleek, tight spaces of Bin 26 Enoteca. On a weeknight, laughter reverberates as waiters carrying plates and bottles of wine weave their way through tables, past the line forming along the entrance. A couple at the bar chats as they study the wine selections with the bartender, and a group of young diners compare neighborhood real estate prices. An urbane scene, and except for the language, it almost could be Rome instead of Beacon Hill. ❖ Azita Bina-Seibel and her brother, Babak, opened Bin 26 in 2006. The two are known for their nearby Persian restaurant, Lala Rokh. But Bina-Seibel, who is the chef, has a long history in Italian cooking — she was one of the original owners of Ristorante Toscano and also owned the former Azita in the South End. ❖ Her dishes are sophisticated, rather spare creations meant to complement wines rather than knock you over. The aim is a simple menu for a casual place with dishes she tries to keep to four ingredients. ❖ Simple doesn't mean boring. A tomato soup has chunky texture and amazing intensity despite being only tomatoes, olive oil, salt, and a few herbs. Slightly runny mozzarella plays off its wrapping of speck (an Italian ham) that's been crisped so its salty taste and crunchy texture hold the cheese and give it verve. An unusual cocoa tagliatelle, a dark tangle of pasta ribbons, is tossed with slivers of porcini. It's spectacular: The pasta gains a depth and texture, but no sweetness, from cocoa, and the porcini buttresses the woodsy, autumnal flavors. And then there's the elusive grace note of calaminth, an Italian cross of oregano and mint. Without meat and only a few elements, this is still a rich and voluptuous dish. ❖ Bina-Seibel's inventiveness carries onto the main courses. Rabbit is stuffed with eggplant that's been sliced like mushrooms, called funghetto-style. The mild rabbit gets a boost from the eggplant and plenty of herbs. Steamed monkfish is sauced with a coffee-laced curry sauce, subtle but adding interest to the meaty fish. Desserts, too, are clever such as the deconstructionist threeramisu with a tiny classic tiramisu, a delicious tiramisu ice cream, and a little tiramisu shake. ❖ The closely placed tables and the noise against the hard surfaces can either make the place feel festive or a little claustrophobic. However, the wait staff seems to work hard to be welcoming even when there's a crowd. And the elegant food, the wine, the ambience make a visit worth the crush.

A.A.

# CLIO (AND UNI)

★★★★⯪

**WEEK 49**

370A Commonwealth Ave., Eliot Hotel,
Boston (Back Bay)
617-536-7200
www.cliorestaurant.com
Major credit cards accepted. Fully accessible.

**PRICES** Clio: appetizers $14-$25,
entrees $30-$44, desserts $11-$24.
Uni: $7-$23, sashimi priced to market.

**HOURS** Dinner: Mon-Fri 5:30-10 p.m.,
Sat-Sun 5:30-10:30 p.m.

**NOISE LEVEL** Padding and careful
spacing mean conversation possible in dining
room and sushi bar.

## MAY WE SUGGEST

Seared hamachi with mushrooms;
duck with chestnut confit; lemon pudding
with chocolate.

TASTING NOTES

_____
_____
_____
_____
_____

**KEN ORINGER** has made a brilliant name as chef of Clio, while often flirting with controversy. The restaurant in the Eliot Hotel has a sophisticated ambience, and the stylish clientele come for his intricate dishes layered with unfamiliar ingredients such as argan oil and bee pollen, emulsions and confetti. But the demurely sized portions — for Boston downright puny — have sometimes caused outcries. And in 2002, he opened Uni, a sashimi bar tucked into a front room — a bold move for a Western chef in a conservative city.

❖ Oringer seems to have grown in control and authority over the years. Clio has always been a well-run place, beautifully appointed without being splashy. The waitstaff manages to be solicitous without hovering. The wine list can be a shock, its prices scaling high, though its selections are seductive.

❖ Oringer's dishes are alluring, too. A server's excitement in telling about hamachi flown in from Japan or a delicate ragout of calamari can make them irresistible. He has a way with texture, slicing the squid so thinly that it resembles angel hair pasta and is just as tender; it's dressed with argan oil and tossed with nasturtiums all sitting in a puddle of carrot emulsion, the sweet and tart elements balancing each other. Many of the entrees here, though, are treated as though they are seasonless. The duck is a tour de force, slices of breast over chestnuts, savory and richly mouth-filling. Oringer fashions the dark meat into a confit that's slightly crisp on the outside and melting in the interior; black radishes add a surprising note of crunch and lychee nuts an interesting sort of sweetness, very clean and understated. Caramelized swordfish "au poivre" rather overdoes the peppering, but a very softly textured blanquette of spiced veal has its seasoning well in hand. The mix of spices creates warmth in the mouth without any one of them jumping out at you. ❖ The finishing touches at Clio are always intriguing. Although there are flights into the trendiest innovations, the best desserts put flavor before chemistry. A chocolate-bedecked lemon pudding comes as a lovely tall cylinder and has a foam-like texture and good citrus flavor. Chicory ice cream on another chocolate dessert has such flowery intrigue on the tongue that I almost ignore the main act. ❖ Oringer has said Uni is his playground, and you can see he is having fun as he composes tiny, pricey masterpieces of raw fish and Kobe beef. It's not the main act at Clio, but it is part of Oringer's dazzle. You won't be bored.

A.A.

# GASLIGHT, BRASSERIE DU COIN

★★☆☆

WEEK
**50**

*560 Harrison Ave., Boston (South End)*
*617-422-0224*
*www.gaslight560.com*
*Major credit cards accepted.*
*Wheelchair accessible.*

**PRICES** *Appetizers: $4.50-$12.50.*
*Entrees: $9-$19.50. Desserts: $6.*

**HOURS** *Mon-Fri 5 p.m.-1:30 a.m.*
*Sat-Sun 10 a.m.-1:30 a.m.*

**NOISE LEVEL** *Very loud.*

## MAY WE SUGGEST

Onion soup; choucroute garni; steak frites;
tarte Tatin.

TASTING NOTES

_____
_____
_____
_____
_____

**WANT TO BET** tarte Tatin's on the dessert menu at Gaslight? You don't. There's no way that textbook French brasserie dessert would have been left out at this textbook French brasserie. At Gaslight, it's not hard to predict what you'll find: Onion soup, steak frites, duck confit, and all your old amis are here. ❖ "Brasserie" means brewery, and Gaslight offers a nice selection of beers, plus French wines in many handy denominations: glass, half-carafe, carafe, or bottle. There are also cocktails with names such as "L'Acolyte" (an excellent, Francofied riff on a sidecar) and "Edith Piaf" (a martini of gin and Lillet Blanc, sure to make you regret beaucoup in the morning). ❖ If descriptions of booze before food go to your head, I apologize. It's simply that Gaslight's cocktails are very good, while its food is pretty good. ❖ The broth in the onion soup could have more depth of flavor, but floating bites of short rib make up for that. Soupe a l'ail with mussels is rich with garlic and a touch of cheese, but quite a few of the mussels are unopened. ❖ In a smoked salmon appetizer, the fish is served with oily, tasteless little cakes that the menu claims are chickpea blini. These are nearly inedible. If you want something from the sea, coquilles St. Jacques is a better bet, the scallops tender and served with pieces of green apple, bacon, and celeriac puree. It's one of the rotating daily specials ❖ Choucroute garni manages to do something theatrical with humble sauerkraut, as waiters arrive bearing a Sterno setup and a cast iron dish. The fermented flavor of the sauerkraut and the rich sausages make a classically delicious pair. ❖ This being a brasserie, there is, of course, steak frites. It's a very good version, chewy and just-past-rare. ❖ As much as food, Gaslight serves the feeling of Frenchness. The space is beautiful, with dark wood ceilings and floors, white tiled walls, and antique mirrors. The restaurant is new, but the zinc bar already gives the feeling of being worn from generations of elbows. In France many of the best-known brasseries are now operated by chains. There's a formula to this kind of restaurant, and Gaslight's got it down. Go for the ambiance, a drink and an affordable bite, and of course the tarte Tatin. It's the first item on the dessert menu, and it, too, is pretty good.

D.F.

# TARANTA

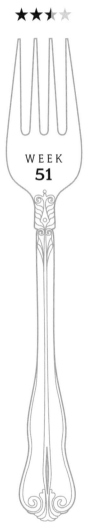

★★⯪☆

WEEK
**51**

210 Hanover St., Boston (North End)
617-720-0052
*www.tarantarist.com*
*MasterCard, Visa, American Express,*
*Diners cards accepted. Street-level dining*
*room with bathrooms downstairs.*

**PRICES** *Antipasti: $9-$16.95.*
*Pasta: $19-$26. Main courses: $25-$34.*
*Desserts: $7.50-$9.50.*

**HOURS** *Nightly 5:30-10 p.m.*

**NOISE LEVEL** *Noisy on busy nights;*
*weeknights quiet.*

## ⋅ MAY WE SUGGEST ⋅

Mini calzones filled with baccala, spicy
beef, and mozzarella; brined double pork
chop with sugar cane, rocoto pepper
glaze; chocolate mousse cake.

**TASTING NOTES**

_____

_____

_____

_____

_____

**WHEN YOU EAT** in the North End, you expect Italian, or at least innovations on Italian themes. What you don't expect is an Italian menu infused with South American ingredients. But that's the charm of Taranta. ❖ Jose Duarte, chef and owner, started out serving Southern Italian cuisine, and then began using ingredients from his native Peru to feed his cooks before the restaurant opened for the evening. Later a few ingredients such as rocoto peppers crept into dishes on the menu. When those met with success, Duarte became bolder, resulting in an intriguing melding of the exotic and more familiar Italian.
❖ Taranta is a homey sort of place, with the cooks working in the open kitchen, extended family groups sharing wine and food, and the waitress telling us about the owner's family visits to Italy. A dinner could begin with an excellent Italian antipasto selection with several types of olives, mozzarella, marinated tomatoes and artichokes, and salami. Add to that an appetizer called calzoncini fritti, a takeoff on calzones that are flaky-crusted South American empanadas; one is filled with salt cod, another with spicy chopped beef, and another with mozzarella and leeks. Served in a clay flowerpot, they're irresistibly crisp and warm. ❖ There are some Southern Italian classics in the pasta section of the menu, but intriguing selections mix it up. Soft pillows of ravioli are filled with ricotta and then sauced with an intense pesto. You can taste the garlic and the pignoli nuts, but the fleeting herbal flavor isn't basil but rather something with an earthier sweetness, a Peruvian black mint. A double pork chop with a glaze of sugar cane and rocoto, a spicy red Peruvian pepper, is accompanied by a saute of big Peruvian white-corn kernels, spinach, and caramelized onions, along with crispy-edged yucca patties, something like another version of corn arepas. Filet mignon with an espresso crust surprises the palate with its slightly bitter edge that marries well with the meat and the sweet-sharp sauce of a Peruvian carob syrup and Italian vincotto (grapes cooked into a syrup-like liquor). ❖ There can be inconsistencies at Taranta, mostly in atmospherics and service — a dining room too warm or cold, and service that ranges from delightful to slow. But a few bites of thoroughly Italian desserts such as a semifreddo of nougat and crunchy praline or an intense chocolate mousse cake smooth out the ending of a meal here. And seeing what Duarte comes up with next in this unusual juxtaposition of Italy and Peru is a reason to return.

A.A.

# DA VINCI

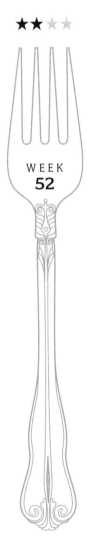

★★ ☆ ☆

WEEK
**52**

*162 Columbus Ave., Boston (Park Square)*
*617-350-0007*
*www.davinciboston.com*
*Major credit cards accepted.*
*Wheelchair accessible.*

**PRICES** *Appetizers: $8-$21.*
*Entrees: $14-$36. Desserts: $8-$12.*

**HOURS** *Mon-Wed 5-10 p.m.*
*Thu-Sat 5-10:30 p.m.*

**NOISE LEVEL** *Loud music, sometimes*
*matched by loud conversation.*

## MAY WE SUGGEST

Pan-seared scallops with artichoke
tapenade; pappardelle; pasta tasting;
veal chop.

TASTING NOTES

**DA VINCI IS IN A** neither-here-nor-there location between the South End and Park Square, a stone's throw from the T yet out of the loop. But city dwellers used to have to drive to Waltham to eat the food of chef Shingara Singh, known (a la Madonna) as Peppino. He used to cook at La Campania.

❖ Peppino was born in India, spent his young adulthood in Germany at an Italian restaurant called Leonardo Da Vinci, then came to the United States. This trajectory isn't visible in his food: Italy is the only land that lands on your plate or in your wineglass. And on many visits, Peppino himself lands at your table, dropping by to say hello and see how your dinner is.

❖ His food is often good and sometimes great. Artichoke tapenade is served perched on a purple radicchio leaf. It's paired with scallops and asparagus spears in an appetizer both lovely and tasty. Pear carpaccio is thin slices of fruit with micro-greens and gorgonzola, sprinkled with pomegranate seeds and a blueberry vinaigrette that grows on the palate.

❖ Da Vinci's pasta is made fresh each day, and it's excellent. Pappardelle are slippery, silky ribbons entangled with sauteed yellow-foot chanterelles, topped with shaved Parmesan and a bit of truffle oil. Gnocchi are so tiny they look like kernels of hominy. They're chewy yet light, topped with similarly sized pieces of buffalo mozzarella and a fresh tomato sauce. You can get the gnocchi on their own or in a pasta tasting with rigatoni Bolognese and half-moon-shaped pasta stuffed with mushrooms, spinach, and ricotta. The Bolognese is first-rate, but the stuffing in the half-moons is bland. ❖ Da Vinci's menu is judiciously small-scale — eight appetizers, four pasta selections, five entrees. It's then augmented by daily specials. On the menu, the veal chop is pink and tender, served with a pleasantly peppery sauce, roasted potatoes, and asparagus. It's much better than the namesake entree, pollo Da Vinci, chicken stuffed with fontina and prosciutto. The dish shines, in a bad way: Everything is covered in a layer of grease, though the bird itself is juicy and nicely cooked. ❖ Tiramisu, creamy and less alcohol-laden than many versions, is accompanied by two strangely crunchy ladyfingers. For a boozier end to the meal, there's the Last Supper, a concoction of Frangelico, Kahlua, and Baileys. Many of the cocktails here have Da Vinci-themed titles. The artist, engineer, musician, and scientist is an interesting figure to name a restaurant for. This, essentially, was a man who could do everything but cook. Fortunately, Peppino's got that part under control.

## BOSTON

*From the Dining Out Hall of Fame archives*

**3**
**EASY**
**STEPS TO**
**BOSTON'S**
**BEST**
**MEALS**

# 1POINT

Go to boston.com/restaurants.

# 2PLAN

Search by cuisine, price or location;
read reviews; make reservations or
get directions.

# 3PIG OUT

Enjoy your meal. And please come again!

# *boston*.com

## For locals. By locals.

**BURP** (optional)
After you've dined, add your own
review to our restaurant listings.